William Eyre

The pope and the people

Select letters and addresses on social questions

William Eyre

The pope and the people
Select letters and addresses on social questions

ISBN/EAN: 9783337104207

Printed in Europe, USA, Canada, Australia, Japan

Cover: Foto ©Lupo / pixelio.de

More available books at **www.hansebooks.com**

THE
POPE AND THE PEOPLE

Select Letters and Addresses on Social Questions

BY HIS HOLINESS
POPE LEO XIII.

EDITED BY THE
REV. W. H. EYRE, S.J.

LONDON AND LEAMINGTON
ART AND BOOK COMPANY
NEW YORK, CINCINNATI, CHICAGO: BENZIGER BROTHERS
1895

NIHIL OBSTAT.

GUL. H. EYRE, S.J.

IMPRIMATUR.

✠ HERBERTUS

CARD: ARCHIEP: WESTMONAST.

Die 21 Decembris, 1894.

PREFACE.

The Encyclical Letters contained in this volume have been chosen out of a large number, as comprising in a special manner the teaching of Leo XIII. on some of the great social questions now agitating the public mind.

Nearly all have already been translated into English. The changes occasionally introduced into existing versions have been made, in the endeavour to render more clear such philosophical and theological terms as, the Editor thought, were too technical to be readily understood by those not familiar with the language of the Schools.

It is scarcely necessary to state that these verbal alterations have been made with permission and approval.

As the Letters can be published separately at a small cost, the Editor would suggest that an exceedingly useful form of charity might be the distribution of some of them on a large scale, notably that "On the Condition of the Working Classes."

114, Mount Street,
    London.
December 20, 1894.

W. H. EYRE, S.J.

CONTENTS.

I.—THE CONDITION OF THE WORKING CLASSES.
(Encyclical Letter, May 15, 1891.) 5.

The Socialist solution ; its refutation—Private Property, a natural right—The right of Private Property proved by the Family—No practical solution without Religion—Labour and suffering must exist—Class must help class—The rich must help the poor—The poor must accept their lot—The Church serves Society by upholding Christianity—She is also solicitous about the temporal interests of her children—The State should promote the general good—should be solicitous for the working population—In what respect the State should interfere—How the State should deal with Labour questions—Working people must have their spiritual rights respected—The State and the regulation of Labour—The Living Wage—The working man should be encouraged to acquire property—Associations and Organizations—The right of Association—The right of Ecclesiastical Association—Bad and dangerous Associations—Catholic Associations for working men to be encouraged—Advice to Catholic Associations—Summary and Conclusion ; Divine Charity 1

II.—ON THE EVILS AFFECTING MODERN SOCIETY, THEIR CAUSES AND REMEDIES.
(Encyclical Letter, April 21, 1878.)

Summary of the evils that affect the human race—These evils are caused by the rejection and contempt of the Church's authority—The Church is the mother of Civil society—Civil society is vain or false if opposed to the Church's teaching and laws—The Apostolic See has deserved well of all Civil society—The country of Italy has most of all experienced the Church's benefits—Restoration of the Holy See to its former dignity and freedom—Union of the whole Catholic flock with the Supreme Pontiff in embracing truth and rejecting error—Observance of God's law about matrimony and the family—Rejoicing on account of union of hearts and minds—Thanks for tokens of obedience received ... 50

III.—THE CHRISTIAN CONSTITUTION OF STATES.
(Encyclical Letter, November 1, 1885.) 2.

The Church is the nursing mother of civilization—Yet she has been traduced from the beginning as an enemy of progress and prosperity in the civil order—An opinion favoured by many nowadays traces the origin of the maxims of social morality to other sources than the teaching of the Church—The modern system of State polity compared with the Christian jurisprudence—Civil society is founded by God, the Author of Nature—Hence God is the source of public authority and of the right to rule—In order to a just and paternal exercise of authority, the sovereign power must take pattern from God—The obedience of subjects for God's sake is honourable and holy—Society, being a moral person, is bound to pay due homage to God—Society is bound, as a consequence, to help its members to attain their last end—Ecclesiastical Society, which is the Church, is instituted by Christ—with a view to the everlasting salvation of souls—The Church is a Universal Society—with a distinction of grades and offices—both natural and supernatural—complete, independent, and supreme—invested with legislative and judicial power—This authority is complete and self-dependent—The twofold authority, that of the Church and that of the civil government, established by God—both of which are confined within certain limits—Between these two powers there exists a certain orderly connection—Sacred things are subject to the authority of the Church—Concordats—The Christian idea of Civil Polity is unexceptionable—Advantages to be derived from the Christian Civil Polity—in both the family and society at large—and in benefit of the social order—St. Augustine enlarges admirably on these benefits—History witnesses to these advantages—The new jurisprudence traced to the revolution of the sixteenth century—the main principle being the false claim of the absolute equality of all men—Whence it follows that the will of the people is looked upon as the sole law—Religious indifference throughout society is openly maintained—also the so-called liberty of conscience—Those who adopt these maxims deny that the Church is a complete society—and seek to sever the affairs of the Church from those of the State—Proofs that this system is at variance with the teachings of reason—Religious indifference—The liberty of the Press—Exclusion of the Church from the business of life, from the school, and from the family—The Church enslaved by the Civil power—Condemnation of these erroneous tenets by the Supreme Pontiffs—The true import of those Papal utterances—Rejection of distorted meanings assigned to them—for instance, the Popes in no wise proscribe any form of government or the toleration of false religions—or reasonable, civil and political liberty—or scientific research—The aim of the Pontiff in renewing this assertion of Catholic truth—Duties of Catholics with reference to opinions—in private life—in their public capacity—Example of the early Christians—Recommendations to Catholics to remain well-affected to the Church, and to be conformed to her mind—to be unanimous in their profession of doctrines taught by the Church—to reject whatever is akin to Naturalism or Rationalism—or divorces public from private duty—foregoing all domestic controversies, especially in the periodical Press ... **65**

IV.—On the Chief Duties of Christians as Citizens.

(Encyclical Letter, January 10, 1890.)

The evil of neglecting Christian teaching—Material progress cannot lead man to his last end—A godless government deserves not the name—Decline of religion owing to the pursuit of tempora advantages—The object of this Encyclical Letter—Catholics, as children of the Church, have imperative duties towards her—The duty of loving the Church and the State—The love of Church and of Country, coming from God, cannot be opposed to each other—The State has no right to order things opposed to God's law—Catholics strictly bound to obey the government in things not conrary to divine authority—Laws invalid which are against those of God—Enmity to Christ and the Church is born of pride—Need of Catholics to be well instructed in their religion—Catholics should be ready and anxious to defend the Faith—To defend the Church is the duty and glory of all Catholics—Catholics should profess and spread the Faith—Faith cometh by hearing, hence the preaching of the word by the Pastors of the Church—Private individuals ought to help in this teaching—Witness of the Vatican Council on this point—Every one bound to preach by example and profession of the Faith—Common action a duty, from the very constitution of the Church—Concord of opinion a prime need—Independence of mind a source of concord even in the natural order—Perfect religious concord is of divine precept—By obedience to the teaching Church revelation is made known to us—Obedience, if not complete, does not exist—St. Thomas of Aquin on the matter—What is included in this complete obedience to the Church—There is no antagonism between Church and State—The Church, exacting obedience from Rulers, helps them to govern—The Church approves of all lawful forms of Civil government—All should imitate the Church in this respect—Civil law must keep in view the moral order—Catholics should uphold Civil Rulers who favour Religion—The enemies of the Church use, against her, dissensions amongst Catholics—Catholic statesmen should shun worldly prudence and rashness—The prudence of the flesh described—How harmful it is to the cause of Christianity—The prudence of the spirit—State prudence consults common good—It concerns above all the Roman Pontiff—then the Bishops—It belongs to the Pope to judge the Rulers of the Church—The chief remedy is to be found in the practice of Christian virtue—The evils threatening nations are the punishment of decay of faith and morals—Charity must be restored towards God and our neighbour —Love of our neighbour carefully preserved amongst the early Christians—How necessary it is in these our times—Warning to parents to bring up their children as true Christians—The nature of Christian training—Commendation of Catholics who have defrayed the expenses of schools—The clergy should exert all their zeal 101

Human Liberty.

(Encyclical Letter, June 20, 1888.)

By Liberty man is master of his actions—Importance of using it aright—What religion has done for Liberty—Modern notions of Liberty—Christian aspect of Liberty—*Natural Liberty*—Man, being rational, is therefore free—The Church has ever upheld this freedom—Its definition—It lies in the will enlightened by reason—The power of choosing evil implies defect in human freedom—*Moral Liberty*—Necessity of law—Natural law, which is our reason commanding us to do good and avoid evil—is identical with the eternal law—Grace is given by God to strengthen and guide the will—but does not hinder freedom—Human law enforces the natural law—and applies its general precepts to particular cases—Hence the eternal law is a standard of true liberty—The Church has ever promoted true freedom—by abolishing slavery and by spreading civilization—by inculcating respect and obedience to lawful authority—by laying down the limits of human authority—Liberalism casts aside authority—Its logical issue—which is repugnant to reason—Its dangerous consequences—Another form of Liberalism limits obedience by the natural law—Its inconsistency—Another form holds that individuals are subject to the Divine law, but not the State—This view is inconsistent with the end of the State—Some false doctrines of Liberalism—*Liberty of Worship*—Man must worship God in the way God wills—in the one true religion—The State is also bound to worship God in a form acceptable to Him—The public profession of Religion is helpful to the liberty of rulers and ruled—*Liberty of the Press* supposes a right to circulate falsehood—*Liberty of Teaching*—Truth, being the perfection of the intellect, can alone be lawfully taught—Natural and supernatural truth cannot be mutually opposed—The teaching of the Church is beneficial to science—and is a safeguard of true freedom—True and false *Liberty of Conscience*—The Church tolerates wrongful teaching for grave reasons—Tolerance of evil a sign of imperfection in the State—Recapitulation of the whole Letter—Various kinds and degrees of Liberalism—Rejection of the Church, or of her claims to have rights—The desire of an impossible compromise—Modern liberties, as they are called, affect dangerous independence—Constitutional forms of government approved by the Church—Also political action for national independence **138**

VI.—Christian Marriage.

(Encyclical Letter, February 10, 1880.)

The restoration of the spiritual order—Many benefits conferred on the natural order itself—both for individual men—and especially for the domestic household—Marriage a divine institution—having from the beginning the two properties of unity and indissolubility—The primitive character of marriage obscured by the Hebrews, through polygamy and divorce; corrupted by the Gentiles with every kind of sin—Jesus Christ restored marriage to its first condition—and raised it to the dignity of a Sacrament—a higher end proposed to nuptial intercourse—The mutual rights and duties of husbands and wives defined—The authority of parents over their children, and reverence of children towards their parents prescribed—The discipline of the marriage state committed by Christ to the Church, which has constantly exercised this divine conferred authority, and has provided by its laws for the due sanctity and protection of marriage—Rationalists have endeavoured to withdraw marriage from the control of the Church, and to treat it as a mere human institution—But the right of the Church to control marriage is seen from the sacred character inherent in it from its first institution—by the dignity of a Sacrament which Christ has willed to apply to it—by the action of our Saviour, of the Apostles, of the Pontiffs and Bishops in its regard—with the united consent of Christian princes—In Christian marriage the contract inseparable from the Sacrament—The evils arising from desecrated marriages considered—These have led to a law of divorce—the fruitful parent of fresh evils—as experience invariably testifies—The Church, by reason of her care to protect the sanctity and perpetuity of the married state, deserves well of nations—The Church, instead of opposing, does greatly aid the Civil power—A concord between both these parties is to be greatly desired—The Pope offers his co-operation to temporal rulers—He strongly exhorts all bishops to urge on the faithful that they ever bear in mind the divine origin of marriage—its supernatural dignity, unity and perpetuity—Mixed marriages to be avoided ... 178

VII.—THE RIGHT ORDERING OF CHRISTIAN LIFE.
(Encyclical Letter, December 30, 1888.)

The Jubilee an occasion of great spiritual benefit to the world—Christian Life—The reign of the threefold lust—Its sources—Bad books and licentious plays—Godless education—The offspring of Godlessness—The remedy being beyond human resource—must come from Jesus Christ—A Christian is bound not to seek after pleasure and fly from labour—The struggle with our passions brings even temporal blessings—The duty of mortification—Prayer—its fruits—Faith restored and increased by prayer—The example of the Clergy—Virtuous nations rewarded with temporal prosperity—The hope of the future is centred in the Church—A prayer for the well-being of the Church 207

VIII.—CONCERNING MODERN ERRORS, SOCIALISM, COMMUNISM, NIHILISM.
(Encyclical Letter, December 28, 1878.)

The character and aims of certain sects described—They attack authority, the family, private property—The source of this rationalism, which since the sixteenth century has invaded the political, scientific, and economical order—The care taken by the Popes to ward off danger by excommunicating members of Secret Societies—The Gospel teachings opposed to Socialism—The Church inculcates obedience of subjects to rulers—and moderation to the rulers of the people—The Church defends the indissoluble union of husband and wife—The Church defines the rights and duties of parents and children, and of masters and servants—It acknowledges the rights of possessing and disposing of private property, honours and relieves the poor, enjoins the rich to give alms—An appeal to peoples and rulers to hearken to the voice of the Church teaching, and to restore liberty to her—Appeal to pastors to plant deep down in the souls of the faithful the teaching of the Church—and to establish Associations of working men—Hope of divine aid 240

IX.—WORKING MEN'S CLUBS AND ASSOCIATIONS.

(An Address to the Officials and Members of the Societies for the Furtherance of Catholic Interests amongst the Industrial Classe in France, February 24, 1885.)

Catholic Working Men's Associations—Self-seeking agitators—The Church and social ills—United action for religious and social ends 241

X.—THE REUNION OF CHRISTENDOM.

(Encyclical Letter, June 20, 1894.)

The Pope's Jubilee and unity amongst Catholics—A great multitude outside Catholic Unity—The Holy Father's concern for those outside Catholic Unity—The most unfortunate of all nations—Former unity amongst civilized nations—The Eastern Churches—Appeal to the Easterns—Appeal to the Slavs—Nations more recently separated drifting into various errors—Catholic Unity and the sure way of salvation—Exhortation to Catholics. .. 245

ERRATA.

Page 11. Line 16. *omit* "who."
,, 24. ,, 3. *for* "afford," *read* "afforded."
,, 73. ,, 21. *omit* "all her affairs."
,, 80. ,, 11. ,, "not."
,, 215. ,, 6. *for* "decree" *read* "degree."
,, 231. ,, 16. ,, "so still" ,, "still so."

THE CONDITION OF THE WORKING CLASSES.

(Encyclical Letter, May 15, 1891.)

THAT the spirit of revolutionary change, which has long been disturbing the nations of the world, should have passed beyond the sphere of politics and made its influence felt in the cognate sphere of practical economics is not surprising. The elements of the conflict now raging are unmistakable, in the vast expansion of industrial pursuits and the marvellous discoveries of science; in the changed relations between masters and workmen; in the enormous fortunes of some few individuals, and the utter poverty of the masses; in the increased self-reliance and closer mutual combination of the working classes; as also, finally, in the prevailing moral degeneracy. The momentous gravity of the state of things now obtaining fills every mind with painful apprehension; wise men are discussing it; practical men are proposing schemes; popular meetings, legislatures, and rulers of nations are all busied with it—and actually there is no question which has taken a deeper hold on the public mind.

Therefore, Venerable Brethren, as on former occasions when it seemed opportune to refute false teaching, we have addressed you in the interests of the Church and of the common weal, and have issued Letters bearing on "Political Power," "Human Liberty," "The Christian Constitution of the State," and like matters, so have we thought it expedient now to speak on THE CONDITION OF THE WORKING CLASSES. It is a subject on which we have already touched more than once, incidentally. But in the present Letter, the responsibility of the Apostolic office urges us to treat the question of set purpose and in detail, in order that no misapprehension may exist as to the principles which truth and justice dictate for its settlement. The discussion is not easy, nor is it void of danger. It is no easy matter to define the relative rights and mutual duties of the rich and of the poor, of Capital and of Labour. And the danger lies in this, that crafty agitators are intent on making use of these differences of opinion to pervert men's judgments and to stir up the people to revolt.

But all agree, and there can be no question whatever, that some remedy must be found, and found quickly, for the misery and wretchedness pressing so heavily and unjustly at this moment on the vast majority of the working classes.

For the ancient working-men's Guilds were abolished in the last century, and no other organisation took their place. Public institutions and the very laws have set aside the ancient religion. Hence by degrees it has come to pass that working-men have been surrendered, all isolated and helpless, to the hard-heartedness of employers and the greed of unchecked competition. The mischief has been increased by rapacious usury, which, although more than once condemned by the Church, is nevertheless, under a different guise, but with the like injustice, still practised by covetous and grasping men. To this must be added the custom of working by contract, and the concentration of so many branches of trade in the hands of a few individuals; so that a small number of very rich men have been able to lay upon the teeming masses of the labouring poor a yoke little better than that of slavery itself.

<small>The 'Socialist solution; its refutation.</small>
To remedy these wrongs the Socialists, working on the poor man's envy of the rich, are striving to do away with private property, and contend that individual possessions should become the common property of all, to be administered by the State or by municipal bodies. They hold that by thus transferring property from private individuals to the community, the present mischievous state of things will be set to rights, inasmuch as each citizen will then get his fair share of whatever there is to enjoy. But their contentions are so clearly powerless to end the controversy that were they carried into effect the working-man himself would be among the first to suffer. They are moreover emphatically unjust, because they would rob the lawful possessor, bring State action into a sphere not within its competence, and create utter confusion in the community.

<small>Private Property a natural right.</small>
It is surely undeniable that, when a man engages in remunerative labour, the impelling reason and motive of his work is to obtain property, and thereafter to hold it as his very own. If one man hires out to another his strength or skill, he does so for the purpose of receiving in return what is necessary for sustenance and education; he therefore expressly intends to acquire a right full and real, not only

to the remuneration, but also to the disposal of such remuneration, just as he pleases. Thus, if he lives sparingly, saves money, and, for greater security, invests his savings in land, the land, in such case, is only his wages under another form; and, consequently, a working-man's little estate thus purchased should be as completely at his full disposal as are the wages he receives for his labour. But it is precisely in such power of disposal that ownership obtains, whether the property consist of land or chattels. Socialists, therefore, by endeavouring to transfer the possessions of individuals to the community at large, strike at the interests of every wage-earner, since they would deprive him of the liberty of disposing of his wages, and thereby of all hope and possibility of increasing his stock and of bettering his condition in life.

What is of far greater moment, however, is the fact that the remedy they propose is manifestly against justice. For every man has by nature the right to possess property as his own. This is one of the chief points of distinction between man and the animal creation, for the brute has no power of self-direction, but is governed by two main instincts, which keep his powers on the alert, impel him to develop them in a fitting manner, and stimulate and determine him to action without any power of choice. One of these instincts is self-preservation, the other the propagation of the species. Both can attain their purpose by means of things which lie within range; beyond their verge the brute creation cannot go, for they are moved to action by their senses only, and in the special direction which these suggest. But with man it is wholly different. He possesses, on the one hand, the full perfection of the animal being, and hence enjoys, at least as much as the rest of the animal kind, the fruition of things material. But animal nature, however perfect, is far from representing the human being in its completeness, and is in truth but humanity's humble handmaid, made to serve and to obey. It is the mind, or reason, which is the predominant element in us who are human creatures; it is this which renders a human being human, and distinguishes him essentially and generically from the brute. And on this very account—that man alone among the animal creation is endowed with reason—it must be within his right to possess things not merely for temporary and momentary use, as other living things do, but to have and to hold them in stable and permanent possession; he must have not only things that perish in the "*user*" but those also which, though they have been reduced into use, continue for further use in after time.

This becomes still more clearly evident if man's nature be considered a little more deeply. For man, fathoming by his faculty of reason matters without number, and linking the future with the present, becoming, furthermore, by taking enlightened forethought, master of his own acts, guides his ways under the eternal law and the power of God, Whose Providence governs all things. Wherefore it is in his power to exercise his choice not only as to matters that regard his present welfare, but also about those which he deems may be for his advantage in time yet to come. Hence man not only can possess the fruits of the earth, but also the very soil, inasmuch as from the produce of the earth he has to lay by provision for the future. Man's needs do not die out, but recur; although satisfied to-day, they demand fresh supplies for to-morrow. Nature accordingly owes to man a storehouse that shall never fail, affording the daily supply for his daily wants. And this he finds solely in the inexhaustible fertility of the earth.

Neither do we, at this stage, need to bring into action the interference of the State. Man precedes the State, and possesses, prior to the formation of any State, the right of providing for the sustenance of his body. Now to affirm that God has given the earth for the use and enjoyment of the whole human race is not to deny that private property is lawful. For God has granted the earth to mankind in general, not in the sense that all without distinction can deal with it as they like, but rather that no part of it has been assigned to anyone in particular, and that the limits of private possession have been left to be fixed by man's own industry, and by the laws of individual races. Moreover, the earth, even though apportioned among private owners, ceases not thereby to minister to the needs of all, inasmuch as there is no one who does not sustain life from what the land produces. Those who do not possess the soil, contribute their labour; hence it may truly be said that all human subsistence is derived either from labour on one's own land, or from some toilsome calling which is paid for either in the produce of the land itself, or in that which is exchanged for what the land brings forth.

Here, again, we have further proof that private ownership is in accordance with the law of nature. Truly, that which is required for the preservation of life, and for life's well-being, is produced in great abundance from the soil, but not until man has brought it into cultivation and expended upon it his solicitude and skill. Now, when man thus turns the activity of his mind and the strength of his body towards procuring the fruits of nature, by such act he makes his own that portion of nature's field which he cultivates—that portion on which he leaves, as it were, the impress of his individuality; and it cannot but be just that he should possess that portion as his very own, and have a right to hold it without any one being justified in violating that right.

So strong and convincing are these arguments, that it seems amazing that some should now be setting up anew certain obsolete opinions in opposition to what is here laid down. They assert that it is right for private persons to have the use of the soil and its various fruits, but that it is unjust for anyone to possess outright either the land on which he has built, or the estate which he has brought under cultivation. But those who deny these rights do not perceive that they are defrauding man of what his own labour has produced. For the soil which is tilled and cultivated with toil and skill utterly changes its condition: it was wild before, now it is fruitful; was barren, but now brings forth in abundance. That which has thus altered and improved the land becomes so truly part of itself as to be in great measure indistinguishable and inseparable from it. Is it just that the fruit of a man's own sweat and labour should be possessed and enjoyed by anyone else? As effects follow their cause, so is it just and right that the results of labour should belong to those who have bestowed their labour.

With reason, then, the common opinion of mankind, little affected by the few dissentients who have contended for the opposite view, has found in the careful study of nature, and in the laws of nature, the foundations of the division of property, and the practice of all ages has consecrated the principle of private ownership, as being pre-eminently in conformity with human nature, and as conducing in the most unmistakable manner to the peace and tranquillity of human existence. The same principle is confirmed and enforced by the civil laws—laws which, so long as they are just, derive from the law of nature their binding force. The authority of the Divine Law adds its sanction, forbidding us in severest terms even to covet that which is another's:—*Thou shalt not covet thy neighbour's wife; nor his house, nor his field, nor his man-servant, nor his maid-servant, nor his ox, nor his ass, nor anything which is his.**

<small>The right of Private Property proved by the Family.</small> The rights here spoken of, belonging to each individual man, are seen in much stronger light when considered in relation to man's social and domestic obligations. In choosing a state of life, it is indisputable that all are at full liberty to follow the counsel of Jesus Christ as to observing virginity, or to bind themselves by the marriage tie. No human law can abolish the natural and original right of marriage, nor in any way limit the chief and principal purpose of marriage, ordained by God's authority from the beginning. *Increase and multiply.*† Hence we have the Family; the "society" of a man's house,—a society limited indeed in numbers, but no less a true "society," anterior to every kind of State or nation, invested with rights and duties of its own, totally independent of the civil community.

---

* *Deuteronomy* v. 21.   † *Genesis* i. 28.

That right of property, therefore, which has been proved to belong naturally to individual persons, must in like wise belong to a man in his capacity of head of a family; nay, such person must possess this right so much the more clearly in proportion as his position multiplies his duties. For it is a most sacred law of nature that a father should provide food and all necessaries for those whom he has begotten; and, similarly, nature dictates that a man's children, who carry on, so to speak, and continue his own personality, should be by him provided with all that is needful to enable them to keep themselves honourably from want and misery amid the uncertainties of this mortal life. Now in no other way can a father effect this except by the ownership of lucrative property, which he can transmit to his children by inheritance. A family, no less than a State, is, as we have said, a true society, governed by a power within its sphere, that is to say, by the father. Provided, therefore, the limits which are prescribed by the very purposes for which it exists be not transgressed, the Family has at least equal rights with the State in the choice and pursuit of the things needful to its preservation and its just liberty.

We say, at least equal rights; for inasmuch as the domestic household is antecedent, as well in idea as in fact, to the gathering of men into a community, the family must necessarily have rights and duties which are prior to those of the Community, and founded more immediately in nature. If the citizens of a State—in other words the families—on entering into association and fellowship, were to experience at the hands of the State hindrance instead of help, and were to find their rights attacked instead of being upheld, such association should be held in detestation, rather than be an object of desire.

The contention, then, that the civil government should at its option intrude into and exercise intimate control over the Family and the household, is a great and pernicious error. True, if a family finds itself in exceeding distress, utterly deprived of the counsel of friends, and without any prospect of extricating itself, it is right that extreme necessity be met by public aid, since each family is a part of the commonwealth. In like manner, if within the precincts of the household there occur grave disturbance of mutual rights, public authority should intervene to force each party to yield to the other its proper due; for this is not to deprive citizens of their rights, but justly and properly to safeguard and strengthen them. But the rulers of the State must go no further: here nature bids them stop. Paternal authority can be neither abolished nor absorbed by the State; for it has the same source as human life itself. "The child belongs to the father," and is, as it were, the continuation of the father's personality; and, speaking strictly, the child takes its place in civil society, not of its own right, but in its quality as member of the family in which it is born. And for the very reason that "the child belongs to the father," it is, as St. Thomas of Aquin says, "before it attains the use of free-will, under power and charge of its parents."* The Socialists, therefore, in setting aside the parent and setting up a State supervision, act *against natural justice*, and break into pieces the stability of all family life.

And not only is such interference unjust, but it is quite

---

* St. Thomas, *Summa Theologica*, 2a 2æ Q. x. Art. 12.

certain to harass and worry all classes of citizens, and subject them to odious and intolerable bondage. It would throw open the door to envy, to mutual invective, and to discord; the sources of wealth themselves would run dry, for no one would have any interest in exerting his talents or his industry; and that ideal equality about which they entertain pleasant dreams would be in reality the levelling down of all to a like condition of misery and degradation.

Hence it is clear that the main tenet of Socialism, community of goods, must be utterly rejected, since it only injures those whom it would seem meant to benefit, is directly contrary to the natural rights of mankind, and would introduce confusion and disorder into the commonweal. The first and most fundamental principle, therefore, if one (who) would undertake to alleviate the condition of the masses, must be the inviolability of private property. This being established, we proceed to show where the remedy sought for must be found.

No practical solution without Religion.

We approach the subject with confidence, and in the exercise of the rights which manifestly appertain to us, for no practical solution of this question will be found apart from the intervention of Religion and of the Church. It is We who are the chief guardian of Religion and the chief dispenser of what pertains to the Church, and We must not by silence neglect the duty incumbent on us. Doubtless this most serious question demands the attention and the efforts of others besides ourselves—to wit, of the rulers of States, of employers of labour, of the wealthy, aye, of the working classes themselves, for whom We are pleading. But We affirm without hesitation that all the striving of men will be vain if they leave out the Church. It is the Church that insists, on the authority of the Gospel, upon those teachings whereby the conflict can be brought to an end, or rendered, at least, far less bitter; the Church uses her efforts not only to enlighten the mind, but to direct by her precepts the life and conduct of each and all; the Church improves and betters the condition of the working-man by means of numerous useful organisations; does her best to enlist the services of all ranks in discussing and endeavouring to meet, in the most practical way, the claims of the working classes; and acts from the positive view that for these purposes recourse should be had, in due measure and degree, to the intervention of the law and of State authority.

Labour and suffering must exist. Let it, then, be taken as granted, in the first place, that the condition of things human must be endured, for it is impossible to reduce civil society to one dead level. Socialists may in that intent do their utmost, but all striving against nature is in vain. There naturally exist among mankind manifold differences of the most important kind; people differ in capacity, skill, health, strength; and unequal fortune is a necessary result of unequal condition. Such inequality is far from being disadvantageous either to individuals or to the community. Social and public life can only be maintained by means of various kinds of capacity for business and the playing of many parts; and each man, as a rule, chooses the part which suits his own peculiar domestic condition. As regards bodily labour, even had man never fallen from *the state of innocence*, he would not have remained wholly unoccupied; but that which would then have been his free choice and his delight, became afterwards compulsory, and the painful expiation for his disobedience. *Cursed be the earth in thy work; in thy labour thou shalt eat of it all the days of thy life.** In like manner, the other pains and hardships of life will have no end or cessation on earth; for the consequences of sin are bitter and hard to bear, and they must accompany man so long as life lasts. To suffer and to endure, therefore, is the lot of humanity; let them strive as they may, no strength and no artifice will ever succeed in banishing from human life the ills and troubles which beset it. If any there are who pretend differently—who hold out to a hard-pressed people the boon of freedom from pain and trouble, an undisturbed repose, and constant enjoyment—they delude the people and impose upon them, and their lying promises will only one day bring forth evils worse than the present. Nothing is more useful than to look upon the world as it really is— and at the same time to seek elsewhere, as we have said, for the solace to its troubles.

Class should help class.

The great mistake made in regard to the matter now under consideration, is to take up with the notion that class is naturally hostile to class, and that the wealthy and the working-men are intended by nature to live in mutual conflict. So irrational and so false is this view, that the direct contrary is the truth. Just as the symmetry of the human frame is the resultant of the disposition of the bodily members, so in a State is it ordained by nature that these two

---

* *Genesis* iii. 17.

classes should dwell in harmony and agreement, and should, as it were, groove into one another, so as to maintain the balance of the body politic. Each needs the other: Capital cannot do without Labour, nor Labour without Capital. Mutual agreement results in pleasantness of life and the beauty of good order; while perpetual conflict necessarily produces confusion and savage barbarity. Now, in preventing such strife as this, and in uprooting it, the efficacy of Christian institutions is marvellous and manifold. First of all, there is no intermediary more powerful than Religion (whereof the Church is the interpreter and guardian) in drawing the rich, and the poor bread-winners, together, by reminding each class of its duties to the other, and especially of the obligations of justice. Thus Religion teaches the labouring man and the artisan to carry out honestly and fairly all equitable agreements freely entered into; never to injure the property, nor to outrage the person, of an employer; never to resort to violence in defending their own cause, nor to engage in riot or disorder; and to have nothing to do with men of evil principles, who work upon the people with artful promises, and excite foolish hopes which usually end in useless regrets, followed by insolvency. Religion teaches the wealthy owner and the employer that their work-people are not to be accounted their bondsmen; that in every man they must respect his dignity and worth as a man and as a Christian; that labour is not a thing to be ashamed of, if we lend ear to right reason and to Christian philosophy, but is an honourable calling, enabling a man to sustain his life in a way upright and creditable; and that it is shameful and inhuman to treat men like chattels to make money by, or to look upon them merely as so much muscle or physical power. Again, therefore, the Church teaches that, as Religion and things, spiritual and mental, are among the working-man's main concerns, the employer is bound to see that the worker has time for his religious duties; that he be not exposed to corrupting influences and dangerous occasions; and that he be not led away to neglect his home and family, or to squander his earnings. Furthermore, the employer must never tax his work-people beyond their strength, or employ them in work unsuited to their sex or age. His great and principal duty is to give every one a fair wage. Doubtless before deciding whether wages are adequate, many things have to be considered; but wealthy owners and all masters of labour should be mindful of this—that to exercise pressure upon the indigent and the destitute for the sake of gain, and to gather one's profit out of the need of another, is condemned by all laws, human and divine. To defraud anyone of wages that are his due is a crime which cries to the avenging anger of Heaven. *Behold, the hire of the labourers . . . which by fraud hath been kept back by you, crieth aloud; and the cry of them hath entered into the ears of the Lord of Sabaoth.** Lastly, the rich must religiously refrain from cutting down the workmen's earnings, whether by force, by fraud, or by usurious dealing; and with all the greater reason because the labouring man is, as a rule, weak and unprotected, and because his slender means should in proportion to their scantiness be accounted sacred.

Were these precepts carefully obeyed and followed out, would they not be sufficient of themselves to keep under all strife and all its causes?

---

* *St. James* v. 4.

The Rich must help the Poor.

But the Church, with Jesus Christ as her Master and Guide, aims higher still. She lays down precepts yet more perfect, and tries to bind class to class in friendliness and good feeling. The things of earth cannot be understood or valued aright without taking into consideration the life to come, the life that will know no death. Exclude the idea of futurity, and forthwith the very notion of what is good and right would perish; nay, the whole scheme of the universe would become a dark and unfathomable mystery. The great truth which we learn from Nature herself is also the grand Christian dogma on which Religion rests as on its foundation—that when we have given up this present life, then shall we really begin to live. God has not created us for the perishable and transitory things of earth, but for things heavenly and everlasting; He has given us this world as a place of exile, and not as our abiding-place. As for riches and the other things which men call good and desirable, whether we have them in abundance, or lack them altogether—so far as eternal happiness is concerned—it matters little; the only important thing is to use them aright. Jesus Christ, when He redeemed us with *plentiful redemption*,* took not away the pains and sorrows which in such large proportion are woven together in the web of our mortal life. He transformed them into motives of virtue and occasions of merit: and no man can hope for eternal reward unless he follow in the blood-stained footprints of his Saviour. *If we suffer with Him, we shall also reign with Him.*† Christ's labours and sufferings, accepted of His own free-will, have marvellously sweetened all

---

* 2 *Timothy* ii. 12.   † 2 *Corinthians* iv. 17.

suffering and all labour. And not only by His example, but by His grace and by the hope held forth of everlasting recompense, has He made pain and grief more easy to endure; *for that which is at present momentary and light of our tribulation, worketh for us above measure exceedingly an eternal weight of glory.* *

Therefore those whom fortune favours are warned that freedom from sorrow and abundance of earthly riches are no warrant for the bliss that shall never end, but rather are obstacles; † that the rich should tremble at the threatenings of Jesus Christ—threatenings so unwonted in the mouth of Our Lord ‡—and that a most strict account must be given to the Supreme Judge for all we possess. The chief and most excellent rule for the right use of money is one which the heathen philosophers hinted at, but which the Church has traced out clearly, and has not only made known to men's minds, but has impressed upon their lives. It rests on the principle that it is one thing to have a right to the possession of money, and another to have a right to use money as one wills. Private ownership, as we have seen, is the natural right of man; and to exercise that right, especially as members of society, is not only lawful, but absolutely necessary. "It is lawful," says St. Thomas of Aquin, "for a man to hold private property; and it is also necessary for the carrying on of human existence." § But if the question be asked, How must one's possessions be used? the Church replies without hesitation in the words of the same holy Doctor: "Man should not consider his outward possessions as his own, but as common to all, so as

---

* 2 *Corinthians* iv. 17.   † *St. Matthew* xix. 23, 24.
‡ *St. Luke* vi. 24, 25.   § 2a 2æ Q. lxvi. Art. 2.

B

to share them without hesitation when others are in need. Whence the Apostle saith, Command the rich of this world . . . to offer with no stint, to apportion largely."* True, no one is commanded to distribute to others that which is required for his own needs and those of his household; nor even to give away what is reasonably required to keep up becomingly his condition in life; "for no one ought to live other than becomingly." † But when what necessity demands has been supplied, and one's standing fairly taken thought for, it becomes a duty to give to the indigent out of what remains over. *Of that which remaineth, give alms.*‡ It is a duty, not of justice (save in extreme cases), but of Christian charity—a duty not enforced by human law. But the laws and judgments of men must yield place to the laws and judgments of Christ the true God, Who in many ways urges on His followers the practice of almsgiving—*It is more blessed to give than to receive;* § and Who will count a kindness done or refused to the poor as done or refused to Himself—*As long as you did it to one of My least brethren, you did it to Me.* ¶ To sum up then what has been said: —Whoever has received from the Divine bounty a large share of temporal blessings, whether they be external and corporeal, or gifts of the mind, has received them for the purpose of using them for the perfecting of his own nature, and, at the same time, that he may employ them, as the steward of God's Providence, for the benefit of others. "He that hath a talent," says St. Gregory the Great, "let him see that he hide it not; he that hath abundance, let him quicken himself to mercy and generosity; he that hath

---

* *Ibid.* Q. lxv. Art. 2. † *Ibid.* Q. xxxii. Art. 6.
‡ *St. Luke* xi. 41. § *Acts* xx. 35. ¶ *St. Matthew* xxv. 40.

art and skill, let him do his best to share the use and the utility thereof with his neighbour." *

The Poor must accept their lot. As for those who possess not the gifts of fortune, they are taught by the Church that in God's sight poverty is no disgrace, and that there is nothing to be ashamed of in seeking one's bread by labour. This is enforced by what we see in Christ Himself, Who *whereas He was rich, for our sakes became poor;*† and Who, being the Son of God, and God Himself, chose to seem and to be considered the son of a carpenter—nay, did not disdain to spend a great part of His life as a carpenter Himself. *Is not this the carpenter, the son of Mary?*‡ From contemplation of this Divine exemplar, it is more easy to understand that the true worth and nobility of man lies in his moral qualities, that is, in virtue; that virtue is moreover the common inheritance of men, equally within the reach of high and low, rich and poor; and that virtue, and virtue alone, wherever found, will be followed by the rewards of everlasting happiness. Nay, God Himself seems to incline rather to those who suffer misfortune; for Jesus Christ calls the poor " blessed;"§ He lovingly invites those in labour and grief to come to Him for solace; ¶ and He displays the tenderest charity towards the lowly and the oppressed. These reflections cannot fail to keep down the pride of those who are well to do, and to embolden the spirit of

---

* St. Gregory the Great, Hom. ix. in *Evangel*. n. 7.
†2 *Corinthians* viii. 9.   ‡ *St. Mark* vi.3.
§ St. Matthew v. 3: *Blessed are the poor in spirit.*   ¶ *Ibid.* xi. 28: *Come to Me all you that labour and are burdened, and I will refresh you.*

the afflicted; to incline the former to generosity and the latter to meek resignation. Thus the separation which pride would set up tends to disappear, nor will it be difficult to make rich and poor join hands in friendly concord.

But, if Christian precepts prevail, the respective classes will not only be united in the bonds of friendship, but also in those of brotherly love. For they will understand and feel that all men are children of the same common Father, Who is God; that all have alike the same last end, which is God Himself, Who alone can make either men or angels absolutely and perfectly happy; that each and all are redeemed and made sons of God, by Jesus Christ, *the first-born among many brethren;* that the blessings of nature and the gifts of grace belong to the whole human race in common, and that from none except the unworthy is withheld the inheritance of the Kingdom of Heaven. *If sons, heirs also; heirs indeed of God, and co-heirs of Christ.* *

The Church serves Society by upholding Christianity.

Such is the scheme of duties and of rights which is shown forth to the world by the Gospel. Would it not seem that, were society penetrated with ideas like these, strife must quickly cease?

But the Church, not content with pointing out the remedy, also applies it. For the Church does her utmost to teach and to train men, and to educate them; and by the intermediary of her bishops and clergy diffuses her salutary teachings far and wide. She strives to influence the mind and the heart so that all may willingly yield themselves to be formed and guided by the commandments of

---

* *Romans* viii. 17.

God. It is precisely in this fundamental and momentous matter, on which everything depends, that the Church possesses a power peculiarly her own. The agencies which she employs are given to her by Jesus Christ Himself for the very purpose of reaching the hearts of men, and derive their efficiency from God. They alone can reach the innermost heart and conscience, and bring men to act from a motive of duty, to resist their passions and appetites, to love God and their fellow-men with a love that is singular and supreme, and to break down courageously every barrier which impedes the way of a life of virtue.

On this subject we need but recall for one moment the examples recorded in history. Of these facts there cannot be any shadow of doubt: for instance, that civil society was renovated in every part by the teachings of Christianity; that in the strength of that renewal the human race was lifted up to better things—nay, that it was brought back from death to life, and to so excellent a life that nothing more perfect had been known before, or will come to be known in the ages that have yet to be. Of this beneficent transformation, Jesus Christ was at once the first cause and the final end; as from Him all came, so to Him was all to be brought back. For when the human race, by the light of the Gospel message, came to know the grand mystery of the Incarnation of the Word and the redemption of man, at once the life of Jesus Christ, God and Man, pervaded every race and nation, and interpenetrated them with His faith, His precepts and His laws. And if Society is to be healed now, in no other way can it be healed save by a return to Christian life and Christian institutions.

When a society is perishing, the wholesome advice to give to those who would restore it is to recall it to the principles from which it sprang; for the purpose and perfection of an association is to aim at and to attain that for which it was formed; and its efforts should be put in motion and inspired by the end and object which originally gave it being. Hence to fall away from its primal constitution implies disease; to go back to it, recovery. And this may be asserted with utmost truth both of the State in general and of that body of its citizens—by far the great majority—who sustain life by their labour.

She is also solicitous about the temporal interest of her children.

Neither must it be supposed that the solicitude of the Church is so pre-occupied with the spiritual concerns of her children as to neglect their temporal and earthly interests. Her desire is that the poor, for example, should rise above poverty and wretchedness, and better their condition in life; and for this she makes a strong endeavour. By the very fact that she calls men to virtue and forms them to its practice, she promotes this in no slight degree. Christian morality, when adequately and completely practised, leads of itself to temporal prosperity, for it merits the blessing of that God Who is the source of all blessings; it powerfully restrains the greed of possession and the thirst for pleasure—twin plagues, which too often make a man who is void of self-restraint, miserable in the midst of abundance;* it makes men supply for the lack of means through economy, teaching them to be content with frugal living, and further, keeping them out of the reach of those vices which devour

---

* *The desire of money is the root of all evils*—1 *Tim.* vi. 10.

not small incomes merely, but large fortunes, and dissipate many a goodly inheritance.

The Church, moreover, intervenes directly in behalf of the poor, by setting on foot and maintaining many associations which she knows to be efficient for the relief of poverty. Herein again she has always succeeded so well as to have even extorted the praise of her enemies. Such was the ardour of brotherly love among the earliest Christians that numbers of those who were in better circumstances, despoiled themselves of their possessions in order to relieve their brethren; whence *neither was there any one needy among them.* * To the order of Deacons, instituted in that very intent, was committed by the Apostles the charge of the daily doles; and the Apostle Paul, though burdened with the solicitude of all the churches, hesitated not to undertake laborious journeys in order to carry the alms of the faithful to the poorer Christians. Tertullian calls these contributions, given voluntarily by Christians in their assemblies, deposits of piety ; because, to cite his own words, they were employed " in feeding the needy, in burying them, in the support of youths and maidens destitute of means and deprived of their parents, in the care of the aged, and the relief of the shipwrecked." †

Thus by degrees came into existence the patrimony which the Church has guarded with religious care as the inheritance of the poor. Nay, to spare them the shame of begging, the common Mother of rich and poor has exerted herself to gather together funds for the support of the needy. The Church has aroused everywhere the heroism of charity, and has established congregations of Religious

---

* *Acts* iv. 34.   † *Apologia Secunda*, xxxix.

and many other useful institutions for help and mercy, so that hardly any kind of suffering could exist which was not afforded relief. At the present day many there are who, like the heathen of old, seek to blame and condemn the Church for such eminent charity. They would substitute in its stead a system of relief organised by the State. But no human expedients will ever make up for the devotedness and self-sacrifice of Christian charity. Charity, as a virtue, pertains to the Church; for virtue it is not, unless it be drawn from the Sacred Heart of Jesus Christ; and whosoever turns his back on the Church cannot be near to Christ.

It cannot, however, be doubted that to attain the purpose we are treating of, not only the Church, but all human agencies must concur. All who are concerned in the matter should be of one mind and according to their ability act together. It is with this, as with the Providence that governs the world; the results of causes do not usually take place save where all the causes co-operate.

The State should promote the general good; It is sufficient therefore, to inquire what part the State should play in the work of remedy and relief.

By the State we here understand, not the particular form of government prevailing in this or that nation, but the State as rightly apprehended; that is to say, any government conformable in its institutions to right reason and natural law, and to those dictates of the Divine wisdom which we have expounded in the Encyclical on "The Christian Constitution of the State." The foremost duty, therefore, of the rulers of the State should be to make sure that the laws and institutions, the general character and administration of the commonwealth, shall be such as of themselves to realise public well-being and private prosperity. This is the proper scope of wise statesmanship and is the work of the heads of the State. Now, a state chiefly prospers and thrives through moral rule, well-regulated family life, respect for religion and justice, the moderation and equal allocation of public taxes, the progress of the arts and of trade, the abundant yield of the land —through everything, in fact, which makes the citizens better and happier. Hereby, then, it lies in the power of a ruler to benefit every class in the State, and amongst the rest to promote to the utmost the interests of the poor; and this in virtue of his office, and without being open to any suspicion of undue interference—since it is the province of the State to consult the common good. And the more that is done for the benefit of the working classes by the general laws of the country, the less need will there be to seek for special means to relieve them.

should be solicitous for the working population.

There is another and deeper consideration which must not be lost sight of. As regards the State, the interests of all, whether high or low, are equal. The poor are members of the national community equally with the rich; they are real component living members which constitute, through the family, the living body; and it need hardly be said that they are in every State very largely in the majority. It would be irrational to neglect one portion of the citizens and favour another; and therefore the public administration must duly and solicitously provide for the welfare and the comfort of the working classes; otherwise that law of justice will be violated which ordains that each man shall have his due. To cite the wise words of St. Thomas of Aquin : " As the part and the whole are in a certain sense identical, the part may in some sense claim what belongs to the whole."* Among the many and grave duties of rulers who would do their best for the people, the first and chief is to act with strict justice—with that justice which is called by the Schoolmen *distributive*—towards each and every class alike.

But although all citizens, without exception, can and ought to contribute to that common good in which individuals share so advantageously to themselves, yet it should not be supposed that all can contribute in the like way and to the same extent. No matter what changes may occur in forms of government, there will ever be differences and inequalities of condition in the State. Society cannot exist or be conceived of without them. Some there must be who devote themselves to the work of the commonwealth, who make the laws or administer justice, or whose advice and authority govern the nation in times of peace, and defend it in war. Such men clearly occupy the foremost place in the State, and should be held in highest estimation, for their work concerns most nearly and effectively the general interests of the community. Those who labour at a trade or calling do not promote the general welfare in such measure as this; but they benefit the nation, if less directly, in a most important manner. Still we have insisted that, since the end of Society is to make men better, the chief good that Society can possess is Virtue. Nevertheless, in all well-constituted States it is in no wise a matter of small moment to provide those bodily and external

---

* 2a 2æ Q. lxi. Art. 1 nd 2.

commodities *the use of which is necessary to virtuous action.**
And in order to provide such material well-being, the labour of the poor—the exercise of their skill, and the employment of their strength, in the culture of the land and in the workshops of trade—is of great account and quite indispensable. Indeed, their co-operation is in this respect so important that it may be truly said that it is only by the labour of working-men that States grow rich. Justice, therefore, demands that the interests of the poorer classes should be carefully watched over by the administration, so that they who contribute so largely to the advantage of the community may themselves share in the benefits which they create—that being housed, clothed, and enabled to sustain life, they may find their existence less hard and more endurable. It follows that whatever shall appear to prove conducive to the well-being of those who work, should obtain favourable consideration. Let it not be feared that solicitude of this kind will be harmful to any interest; on the contrary, it will be to the advantage of all; for it cannot but be good for the commonwealth to shield from misery those on whom it so largely depends.

In what respects the State should interfere. We have said that the State must not absorb the individual or the family; both should be allowed free and untrammelled action so far as is consistent with the common good and the interests of others. Rulers should, nevertheless, anxiously safeguard the community and all its members: the community, because the conservation thereof is so emphatically the business of the supreme

---
* St. Thomas of Aquin, *De Regimine Principum*, i. 15.

power, that the safety of the commonwealth is not only the first law, but it is a Government's whole reason of existence; and the members, because both philosophy and the Gospel concur in laying down that the object of the government of the State should be, not the advantage of the ruler, but the benefit of those over whom he is placed. The gift of authority derives from God, and is, as it were, a participation in the highest of all sovereignties; and should be exercised as the power of God is exercised—with a fatherly solicitude which not only guides the whole, but reaches also to details.

Whenever the general interest or any particular class suffers, or is threatened with mischief which can in no other way be met or prevented, the public authority must step in to deal with it. Now, it interests the public, as as well as the individual, that peace and good order should be maintained; that family life should be carried on in accordance with God's laws and those of nature; that Religion should be reverenced and obeyed; that a high standard of morality should prevail, both in public and private life; that the sanctity of justice should be respected, and that no one should injure another with impunity; that the members of the commonwealth should grow up to man's estate strong and robust, and capable, if need be, of guarding and defending their country. If by a strike, or other combination of workmen, there should be imminent danger of disturbance to the public peace; or if circumstances were such as that among the labouring population the ties of family life were relaxed; if Religion were found to suffer through the operatives not having time and opportunity afforded them to practise its duties; if in workshops and factories there were danger to morals through the mixing of the sexes or from other harmful occasions of evil; or if employers laid burdens upon their workmen which were unjust, or degraded them with conditions repugnant to their dignity as human beings; finally, if health were endangered by excessive labour, or by work unsuited to sex or age—in such cases, there can be no question but that, within certain limits, it would be right to invoke the aid and authority of the law. The limits must be determined by the nature of the occasion which calls for the law's interference—the principle being that the law must not undertake more, nor proceed further, than is required for the remedy of the evil or the removal of the mischief.

Rights must be religiously respected wherever they exist; and it is the duty of the public authority to prevent and to punish injury, and to protect every one in the possession of his own. Still, when there is question of defending the rights of individuals, the poor and helpless have a claim to especial consideration. The richer class have many ways of shielding themselves, and stand less in need of help from the State; whereas those who are badly off have no resources of their own to fall back upon, and must chiefly depend upon the assistance of the State. And it is for this reason that wage-earners, who are undoubtedly among the weak and necessitous, should be specially cared for and protected by the Government.

How the State should deal with labour questions. Here, however, it is expedient to bring under special notice certain matters of moment. It should ever be borne in mind that the chief thing to be realised is the safe-guarding of private property by legal enactment and public policy. Most of all is it essential amid such a fever of excitement, to keep the multitude within the line of duty; for if all may justly strive to better their condition, neither justice nor the common good allows any individual to seize upon that which belongs to another, or, under the futile and shallow pretext of equality, to lay violent hands on other people's possessions. Most true it is that by far the larger part of the workers prefer to better themselves by honest labour rather than by doing any wrong to others. But there are not a few who are imbued with evil principles and eager for revolutionary change, whose main purpose is to stir up tumult and bring about measures of violence. The authority of the State should intervene to put restraint upon such fire-brands, to save the working classes from their seditious arts, and protect lawful owners from spoliation.

When work-people have recourse to a strike, it is frequently because the hours of labour are too long, or the work too hard, or because they consider their wages insufficient. The grave inconvenience of this not uncommon occurrence should be obviated by public remedial measures; for such paralyzing of labour not only affects the masters and their work-people alike, but is extremely injurious to trade and to the general interests of the public; moreover, on such occasions, violence and disorder are generally not far distant, and thus it frequently happens that the public peace is imperilled. The laws should forestal and prevent such troubles from arising;

they should lend their influence and authority to the removal in good time of the causes which lead to conflicts between employers and employed.

Working people must have their spiritual rights respected.

But if owners of property should be made secure, the working-man, in like manner has property and belongings in respect to which he should be protected; and foremost of all, his soul and mind. Life on earth, however good and desirable in itself, is not the final purpose for which man is created; it is only the way and the means to that attainment of truth and that practice of goodness in which the full life of the soul consists. It is the soul which is made after the image and likeness of God; it is in the soul that the sovereignty resides in virtue whereof man is commanded to rule the creatures below him and to use all the earth and the ocean for his profit and advantage. *Fill the earth and subdue it; and rule over the fishes of the sea, and the fowls of the air, and all living creatures which move upon the earth.** In this respect all men are equal; there is no difference between rich and poor, master and servant, ruler and ruled, *for the same is Lord over all.*† No man may with impunity outrage that human dignity which God Himself treats *with reverence*, nor stand in the way of that higher life which is the preparation for the eternal life of Heaven. Nay, more; no man has in this matter power over himself. To consent to any treatment which is calculated to defeat the end and purpose of his being is beyond his right; he cannot give up his soul to servitude; for it is not

---

* *Genesis* i. 28.   † *Romans* x. 12.

man's own rights which are here in question, but the rights of God, the most sacred and inviolable of rights. From this follows the obligation of the cessation from work and labour on Sundays and certain holydays. The rest from labour is not to be understood as mere giving way to idleness; much less must it be an occasion for spending money and for vicious indulgence, as many would have it to be; but it should be rest from labour, hallowed by religion. Rest (combined with religious observances), disposes man to forget for a while the business of this every-day life, to turn his thoughts to things heavenly, and to the worship which he so strictly owes to the Eternal Godhead. It is this, above all, which is the reason and motive of Sunday rest; a rest sanctioned by God's great law of the Ancient Covenant—*Remember thou keep holy the Sabbath day*,* and taught to the world by His own mysterious "rest" after the creation of man: *He rested on the seventh day from all His work which He had done.*†

The State and the regulation of Labour.

If we turn now to things external and corporeal, the first concern of all is to save the poor workers from the cruelty of greedy speculators, who use human beings as mere instruments for money-making. It is neither just nor human so to grind men down with excessive labour as to stupefy their minds and wear out their bodies. Man's powers, like his general nature, are limited, and beyond these limits he cannot go. His strength is developed and increased by use and exercise, but only on condition of due intermission and proper rest. Daily labour, therefore, should be so regulated as not to be

---

* *Exod.* xx. 8.   † *Genesis* ii. 2.

protracted over longer hours than strength admits. How many and how long the intervals of rest should be, must depend on the nature of the work, on circumstances of time and place, and on the health and strength of the workman. Those who work in mines and quarries, and extract coal, stone, and metals from the bowels of the earth, should have shorter hours in proportion as their labour is more severe and trying to health. Then, again, the season of the year should be taken into account; for not unfrequently a kind of labour is easy at one time which at another is intolerable or exceedingly difficult. Finally, work which is quite suitable for a strong man cannot reasonably be required from a woman or a child. And, in regard to children, great care should be taken not to place them in work-shops and factories until their bodies and minds are sufficiently developed. For just as very rough weather destroys the buds of spring, so does too early an experience of life's hard toil blight the young promise of a child's faculties, and render any true education impossible. Women, again, are not suited for certain occupations; a woman is by nature fitted for home-work, and it is that which is best adapted at once to preserve her modesty and to promote the good bringing-up of children and the well-being of the family. As a general principle it may be laid down that a workman ought to have leisure and rest proportionate to the wear and tear of his strength; for waste of strength must be repaired by cessation from hard work.

In all agreements between masters and work-people, there is always the condition expressed or understood that there should be allowed proper rest for soul and body.

To agree, in any other sense, would be against what is right and just; for it can never be just or right to require on the one side, or to promise on the other, the giving up of those duties which a man owes to his God and to himself.

The Living Wage. We now approach a subject of great and urgent importance, and one in respect of which, if extremes are to be avoided, right notions are absolutely necessary. Wages, as we are told, are regulated by free consent, and therefore the employer, when he pays what was agreed upon, has done his part and seemingly is not called upon to do anything beyond. The only way, it is said, in which injustice might occur would be if the master refused to pay the whole of the wages, or if the workman should not complete the work undertaken; in such cases the State should intervene, to see that each obtains his due:—but not under any other circumstances.

This mode of reasoning is, to a fair-minded man, by no means convincing, for there are important considerations which it leaves out of account altogether. To labour is to exert oneself for the sake of procuring what is necessary for the purposes of life, and chief of all for self-preservation. *In the sweat of thy brow thou shalt eat thy bread.** Hence a man's labour bears two notes or characters. First of all, it is _personal_, inasmuch as the exertion of individual strength belongs to the individual who puts it forth, employing such strength to procure that personal advantage on account of which it was bestowed. Secondly, man's labour is _necessary;_ for without

---

* *Genesis* iii. 19.

the result of labour a man cannot live; and self-preservation is a law of Nature, which it is wrong to disobey. Now, were we to consider labour so far as it is *personal* merely, doubtless it would be within the workman's right to accept any rate of wages whatsoever; for in the same way as he is free to work or not, so is he free to accept a small remuneration or even none at all. But this is a mere abstract supposition; the labour of the workingman is not only his personal attribute, but it is *necessary*; and this makes all the difference. The preservation of life is the bounden duty of one and all, and to be wanting therein is a crime. It follows that each one has a right to procure what is required in order to live; and the poor can procure it in no other way than through work and wages.

Let it be then taken for granted, that workman and employer should, as a rule, make free agreements, and in particular should agree freely as to the wages; nevertheless, there underlies a dictate of nature more imperious and more ancient than any bargain between man and man, namely, that the remuneration must be sufficient to support the wage-earner in reasonable and frugal comfort. If through necessity or fear of a worse evil the workman accept harder conditions because an employer or contractor will afford him no better, he is made the victim of force and injustice. In these and similar questions, however—such as, for example, the hours of labour in different trades, the sanitary precautions to be observed in factories and workshops, etc.—in order to supersede undue interference on the part of the State, especially as circumstances, times, and localities differ so widely, it is advisable that recourse be had to Societies or Boards such as We shall mention presently, or to some other mode of safeguarding the interests of the wage-earners; the State being appealed to, should circumstances require, for its sanction and protection.

The working-man should be encouraged to acquire property.

If a workman's wages be sufficient to enable him to maintain himself, his wife, and his children in reasonable comfort, he will not find it difficult, if he be a sensible man, to study economy; and he will not fail, by cutting down expenses, to put by some little savings and thus secure a small income. Nature and reason alike would urge him to this. We have seen that this great Labour-question cannot be solved save by assuming as a principle that private ownership must be held sacred and inviolable. The law, therefore, should favour ownership, and its policy should be to induce as many as possible of the humbler class to become owners.

Many excellent results will follow from this; and first of all, property will certainly become more equitably divided. For the result of civil change and revolution has been to divide society into two widely-differing castes. On the one side there is the party which holds power because it holds wealth; which has in its grasp the whole of labour and trade; which manipulates for its own benefit and its own purposes all the sources of supply, and which is even represented in the councils of the State itself. On the other side there is the needy and powerless multitude, broken-down and suffering, and ever ready for disturbance. If working-people can be encouraged to look forward to obtaining a share in the land, the consequence will be that the gulf between vast wealth and sheer poverty

THE CONDITION OF THE WORKING CLASSES. 37

will be bridged over, and the respective classes will be brought nearer to one another. A further consequence will result in the greater abundance of the fruits of the earth. Men always work harder and more readily when they work on that which belongs to them; nay, they learn to love the very soil that yields, in response to the labour of their hands, not only food to eat, but an abundance of good things for themselves and those that are dear to them. That such a spirit of willing labour would add to the produce of the earth and to the wealth of the community is self-evident. And a third advantage would spring from this: men would cling to the country in which they were born; for no one would exchange his country for a foreign land if his own afforded him the means of living a decent and happy life. These three important benefits, however, can be reckoned on only provided that a man's means be not drained and exhausted by excessive taxation. The right to possess private property is derived from nature, not from man; and the State has the right to control its use in the interests of the public good alone, but by no means to absorb it altogether. The State would therefore be unjust and cruel if under the name of taxation it were to deprive the private owner of more than is fitting.

Associations and organisations. In the last place—employers and workmen may of themselves effect much in the matter we are treating, by means of such associations and organisations as afford opportune aid to those who are in distress, and which draw the two classes more closely together. Among these may be enumerated, societies for mutual help; various benevolent foundations established by private persons to provide for the workman, and for his widow or his orphans, in case of sudden calamity, in sickness, and in the event of death; and what are called "patronages," or institutions for the care of boys and girls, for young people, as well as homes for the aged.

The most important of all are Working-men's Unions; for these virtually include all the rest. History attests what excellent results were brought about by the Artificers' Guilds of olden times. They were the means of affording not only many advantages to the workmen, but in no small degree of promoting the advancement of art, as numerous monuments remain to bear witness. Such Unions should be suited to the requirements of this our age—an age of wider education, of different habits, and of far more numerous requirements in daily life. It is gratifying to know that there are actually in existence not a few Associations of this nature, consisting either of workmen alone, or of workmen and employers together; but it were greatly to be desired that they should become more numerous and more efficient. We have spoken of them more than once; yet it will be well to explain here how notably they are needed, to show that they exist of their own right, and what should be their organisation and their mode of action.

The consciousness of his own weakness urges man to call in aid from without. We read in the pages of Holy Writ: *It is better that two should be together than one; for they have the advantage of their society. If one fall he shall be supported by the other. Woe to him that is alone, for when he falleth he hath none to lift him up.**

---

* *Ecclesiastes* iv. 9, 10.

And further: *A brother that is helped by his brother is like a strong city.* * It is this natural impulse which binds men together in civil society; and it is likewise this which leads them to join together in associations of citizen with citizen; associations which, it is true, cannot be called societies in the full sense of the word, but which, notwithstanding, *are* societies.

The rights of associations.

These lesser societies and the society which constitutes the State differ in many respects, because their immediate purpose and aim is different. Civil society exists for the common good, and hence is concerned with the interests of all in general, albeit with individual interests also in their due place and degree. It is therefore called *public* society, because by its agency, as St. Thomas of Aquin says, "Men establish relations in common with one another in the setting up of a commonwealth."† But societies which are formed in the bosom of the State are styled *private*, and rightly so, since their immediate purpose is the private advantage of the associates. "Now a private society," says St. Thomas again, "is one which is formed for the purpose of carrying out private objects; as when two or three enter into partnership with the view of trading in common."‡ Private societies, then, although they exist within the State, and are severally part of the State, cannot nevertheless be absolutely, and as such, prohibited by the State. For to enter into a "society" of this kind is the natural right of man; and the State is bound to protect natural rights, not to destroy them;

---
* *Proverbs* xviii. 19.
† *Contra impugnantes Dei cultum et religionem*, ii. ‡ *Ibid.*

and if it forbid its citizens to form associations, it contradicts the very principle of its own existence; for both they and it exist in virtue of the like principle, namely, the natural tendency of man to dwell in society.

There are occasions, doubtless, when it is fitting that the law should intervene to prevent association; as when men join together for purposes which are evidently bad, unlawful, or dangerous to the State. In such cases public authority may justly forbid the formation of associations, and may dissolve them if they already exist. But every precaution should be taken not to violate the rights of individuals and not to impose unreasonable regulations under pretence of public benefit. For laws only bind when they are in accordance with right reason, and hence with the eternal law of God.*

The right of ecclesiastical association.

And here we are reminded of the Confraternities, Societies, and Religious Orders which have arisen by the Church's authority and the piety of Christian men. The annals of every nation down to our own days bear witness to what they have accomplished for the human race. It is indisputable that on grounds of reason alone such associations, being perfectly blameless in their objects, possess the sanction of the law of nature. In their religious aspect, they claim rightly to be responsible to the Church alone. The rulers of the State accordingly

---

* "Human law is law only by virtue of its accordance with right reason: and thus it is manifest that it flows from the eternal law. And in so far as it deviates from right reason it is called an unjust law; in such case it is no law at all, but rather a species of violence."
—St. Thomas of Aquin, *Summa Theologica*, 1a 2æ Q. xciii. art. 3.

have no rights over them, nor can they claim any share in their control; on the contrary, it is the duty of the State to respect and cherish them, and, if need be, to defend them from attack. It is notorious that a very different course has been followed, more especially in our own times. In many places the State authorities have laid violent hands on these communities, and committed manifold injustice against them; it has placed them under control of the civil law, taken away their rights as corporate bodies, and despoiled them of their property. In such property the Church had her rights, each member of the body had his or her rights, and there were also the rights of those who had founded or endowed these communities for a definite purpose, and, furthermore, of those for whose benefit and assistance they had their being. Therefore We cannot refrain from complaining of such spoliation as unjust and fraught with evil results; and with all the more reason do We complain because, at the very time when the law proclaims that association is free to all, We see that Catholic Societies, however peaceful and useful, are hampered in every way, whereas the utmost liberty is conceded to individuals whose purposes are at once hurtful to Religion and dangerous to the State.

Bad and dangerous Associations. Associations of every kind, and especially those of working-men, are now far more common than heretofore. As regards many of these there is no need at present to inquire whence they spring, what are their objects, or what the means they employ. There is a good deal of evidence, however, which goes to prove that many of these societies are in the hands of secret leaders, and are managed on principles ill-according with Christianity and the public well-being; and that they do their utmost to get within their grasp the whole field of labour, and force working-men either to join them or to starve. Under these circumstances Christian working-men must do one of two things: either join associations in which their religion will be exposed to peril, or form Associations among themselves—unite their forces and shake off courageously the yoke of so unrighteous and intolerable an oppression. No one who does not wish to expose man's chief good to extreme risk will for a moment hesitate to say that the second alternative should by all means be adopted.

<small>Catholic Associations for working-men to be encouraged.</small>

Those Catholics are worthy of all praise—and they are not a few—who, understanding what the times require, have striven, by various undertakings and endeavours, to better the condition of the working-class without any sacrifice of principle being involved. They have taken up the cause of the working-man, and have spared no efforts to better the condition both of families and individuals; to infuse a spirit of equity into the mutual relations of employers and employed; to keep before the eyes of both classes the precepts of duty and the laws of the Gospel—that Gospel which, by inculcating self-restraint, keeps men within the bounds of moderation, and tends to establish harmony among the divergent interests, and the various classes which compose the State. It is with such ends in view that we see men of eminence meeting together for discussion, for the promotion of concerted action, and for practical work. Others, again, strive to unite working-men of various grades into Associations, help them with their advice and means, and enable them to obtain fitting and profitable employment. The Bishops, on their part, bestow their ready good-will and support; and with their approval and guidance many members of the clergy, both secular and regular, labour assiduously in behalf of the spiritual and mental interests of the members of such Associations. And there are not wanting Catholics blessed with affluence, who have, as it were, cast in their lot with the wage-earners, and who have spent large sums in founding and widely spreading Benefit and Insurance Societies, by means of which the working-man may without difficulty acquire through his labour not only many present advantages, but also the certainty of honourable support in days to come. How greatly such manifold and earnest activity has benefited the community at large is too well known to require Us to dwell upon it. We find therein grounds for most cheering hope in the future, provided always that the Associations We have described continue to grow and spread, and are well and wisely administered. Let the State watch over these Societies of citizens banded together for the exercise of their rights; but let it not thrust itself into their peculiar concerns and their organisation; for things move and live by the spirit inspiring them, and may be killed by the rough grasp of a hand from without.

Advice to Catholic associations. In order then that an Association may be carried on with unity of purpose and harmony of action, its organisation and government should be firm and wise.

All such Societies, being free to exist, have the further right to adopt such rules and organisation as may best conduce to the attainment of their respective objects. We do not judge it expedient to enter into minute particulars touching the subject of organisation: this must depend on national character, on practice and experience, on the nature and aim of the work to be done, on the scope of the various trades and employments, and on other circumstances of fact and of time:—all of which should be carefully considered.

To sum up, then, We may lay it down as a general and lasting law, that working-men's Associations should be so organised and governed as to furnish the best and most suitable means for attaining what is aimed at, that is to say, for helping each individual member to better his condition to the utmost in body, mind, and property. It is clear that they must pay special and chief attention to the duties of religion and morality, and that their internal discipline must be guided very strictly by these weighty considerations; otherwise they would lose wholly their special character, and end by becoming little better than those societies which take no account whatever of Religion. What advantage can it be to a working-man to obtain by means of a Society all that he requires, and to endanger his soul for lack of spiritual food? *What doth it profit a man if he gain the whole world and suffer the loss of his own soul?** This, as Our Lord teaches, is the mark or character that distinguishes the Christian from the heathen. *After all these things do the heathens seek. . . . Seek ye first the Kingdom of God*

---

* *Matthew* xvi. 26.

and His justice, and all these things shall be added unto you.* Let our Associations, then, look first and before all things to God; let religious instruction have therein the foremost place, each one being carefully taught what is his duty to God, what he has to believe, what to hope for, and how he is to work out his salvation : and let all be warned and strengthened with special care against wrong principles and false teaching. Let the working-man be urged and led to the worship of God, to the earnest practice of religion, and, among other things, to the keeping holy of Sundays and holydays. Let him learn to reverence and love Holy Church, the common Mother of us all; and hence to obey the precepts of the Church, and to frequent the Sacraments, since they are the means ordained by God for obtaining forgiveness of sin and for leading a holy life.

The foundations of the organisation being thus laid in Religion, We next proceed to make clear the relations of the members one to another, in order that they may live together in concord and go forward prosperously and with good results. The offices and charges of the Society should be apportioned for the good of the Society itself, and in such mode that difference in degree or standing should not interfere with unanimity and good-will. Office-bearers should be appointed with due prudence and discretion, and each one's charge should be carefully mapped out. Hereby no member will suffer injury. Let the common funds be administered with strict honesty, in such mode that a member may receive assistance in proportion to his necessities. The rights

---
* *Matthew* vi. 32, 33.

and duties of the employers, as compared with the rights and duties of the employed, ought to be the subject of careful consideration. Should it happen that either a master or a workman believe himself injured, nothing would be more desirable than that a committee should be appointed composed of reliable and capable members of the Association, whose duty would be, conformably with the rules of the Association, to settle the dispute. Among the several purposes of a Society, one should be to try to arrange for a continuous supply of work at all times and seasons; as well as to create a fund out of which the members may be effectually helped in their needs, not only in cases of accident, but also in sickness, old age, and distress.

Such rules and regulations, if willingly obeyed by all, will sufficiently ensure the well-being of the poor; whilst such Mutual Associations among Catholics are certain to be productive in no small degree of prosperity to the State. It is not rash to conjecture the future from the past. Age gives way to age, but the events of one century are wonderfully like those of another; for they are directed by the Providence of God, Who over-rules the course of history in accordance with His purposes in creating the race of man. We are told that it was cast as a reproach on the Christians in the early ages of the Church that the greater number among them had to live by begging or by labour. Yet, destitute though they were of wealth and influence, they ended by winning over to their side the favour of the rich and the good-will of the powerful. They showed themselves industrious, hard-working, assiduous, and peaceful, ruled by justice, and, above all, bound together in brotherly love. In presence of such mode of life and such example, prejudice gave way, the tongue of malevolence was silenced, and the lying legends of ancient superstition little by little yielded to Christian truth.

At the time being, the condition of the working classes is the pressing question of the hour; and nothing can be of higher interest to all classes of the State than that it should be rightly and reasonably adjusted. But it will be easy for Christian working-men to decide it aright if they will form Associations, choose wise guides, and follow on the path which with so much advantage to themselves and the commonweal was trodden by their fathers before them. Prejudice, it is true, is mighty, and so is the greed of money; but if the sense of what is just and rightful be not debased through depravity of heart, their fellow-citizens are sure to be won over to a kindly feeling towards men whom they see to be in earnest as regards their work and who prefer so unmistakably right dealing to mere lucre, and the sacredness of duty to every other consideration.

And further great advantage would result from the state of things We are describing; there would exist so much more ground for hope, and likelihood even, of recalling to a sense of their duty those working-men who have either given up their faith altogether, or whose lives are at variance with its precepts. Such men feel in most cases that they have been fooled by empty promises and deceived by false pretexts. They cannot but perceive that their grasping employers too often treat them with great inhumanity and hardly care for them outside the profit their labour brings; and if they belong to any Union, it is probably one in which there exists, in stead of charity and love, that intestine strife which ever accompanies poverty when unresigned and unsustained by religion. Broken in spirit and worn down in body, how many of them would gladly free themselves from such galling bondage! But human respect, or the dread of starvation, makes them tremble to take the step. To such as these, Catholic Associations are of incalculable service, by helping them out of their difficulties, inviting them to companionship, and receiving the returning wanderers to a haven where they may securely find repose.

Summary and Conclusion; Divine Charity. We have now laid before you, Venerable Brethren, both who are the persons, and what are the means whereby this most arduous question must be solved. Every one should put his hand to the work which falls to his share, and that at once and straightway, lest the evil which is already so great become through delay absolutely beyond remedy. Those who rule the State should avail them of the laws and institutions of the country; masters and wealthy owners must be mindful of their duty; the poor, whose interests are at stake, should make every lawful and proper effort; and since religion alone, as We said at the beginning, can avail to destroy the evil at its root, all men should rest persuaded that the main thing needful is to return to real Christianity, apart from which all the plans and devices of the wisest will prove of little avail.

In regard to the Church, her co-operation will never be found lacking, be the time or the occasion what it may; and she will intervene with all the greater effect in proportion as her liberty of action is the more unfettered. Let this be carefully taken to heart by those whose office it is to safeguard the public welfare. Every minister of holy religion must bring to the struggle the full energy of his mind and all his power of endurance. Moved by your authority, Venerable Brethren, and quickened by your example, they should never cease to urge upon men of every class, upon the high-placed as well as the lowly, the Gospel doctrines of Christian life; by every means in their power they must strive to secure the good of the people; and above all must earnestly cherish in themselves, and try to arouse in others, charity, the mistress and the queen of virtues. For the happy results we all long for must be chiefly brought about by the plenteous outpouring of charity; of that true Christian charity which is the fulfilling of the whole Gospel law, which is always ready to sacrifice itself for others' sake, and is man's surest antidote against worldly pride and immoderate love of self; that charity whose office is described and whose Godlike features are outlined by the Apostle St. Paul in these words: *Charity is patient, is kind, ... seeketh not her own, ... suffereth all things, ... endureth all things.**

On each one of you, Venerable Brothers, and on your Clergy and people, as an earnest of God's mercy and a mark of Our affection, We, lovingly in the Lord, bestow the Apostolic Benediction.

---

* 1 *Cor.* xiii. 4—7.

ON THE EVILS AFFECTING MODERN SOCIETY.

THEIR CAUSES AND REMEDIES.

Encyclical Letter, April 21, 1878.

WHEN by God's unsearchable design, We, though all unworthy, were raised to the height of Apostolic dignity, at once We felt Ourselves moved by an urgent desire and, as it were, necessity, to address you by letter, not merely to express to you Our very deep feeling of love, but further, in accordance with the task entrusted to Us from heaven, to strengthen you who are called to share Our solicitude, that you may help Us to carry on the battle now being waged on behalf of the Church of God and the salvation of souls.

Summary of the evils that afflict the human race. For, from the very beginning of Our Pontificate, the sad sight has presented itself to Us of the evils by which the human race is oppressed on every side: the wide-spread subversion of the primary truths on which, as on its foundations, human society is based; the obstinacy of mind, that will not brook any authority however lawful; the endless sources of disagreement, whence arise civil strife, and ruthless war and bloodshed; the contempt of law which moulds characters and is the shield of righteousness; the insatiable craving for things perishable, with complete forgetfulness of things eternal, leading up to the desperate madness whereby so many wretched beings, in all directions, scruple not to lay violent hands upon themselves; the reckless mismanagement, waste and misappropriation of the public funds; the shamelessness of those who, full of treachery, make semblance of being champions of country, of freedom, and every kind of right; in fine, the deadly kind of plague which infects society in its inmost recesses, allowing it no respite, and foreboding ever fresh disturbances and final disaster.

These evils are caused by the rejection and contempt of the Church's authority.

Now the source of these evils lies chiefly, We are convinced, in this, that the holy and venerable authority of the Church, which in God's name rules mankind, upholding and defending all lawful authority, has been despised and set aside. The enemies of public order, being fully aware of this, have thought nothing better suited to destroy the foundations of society than to make an unflagging attack upon the Church of God, to bring her into discredit and odium by spreading infamous calumnies, and accusing her of being opposed to genuine progress. They labour to weaken her influence and power by wounds daily inflicted, and to overthrow the authority of the Bishop of Rome, in whom the abiding and unchangeable principles of right and good find their earthly guardian and champion. From these causes have originated laws that shake the structure of the Catholic Church, the enacting whereof we have to deplore in so many lands; hence too have flowed forth contempt of episcopal authority; the obstacles thrown in the way of the discharge of ecclesiastical duties; the dissolution of religious bodies; and the confiscation of property that was once the support of the Church's ministers and of the poor. Thereby public institutions, vowed to charity and benevolence, have been withdrawn from the wholesome control of the Church; thence also has arisen that unchecked freedom to teach and spread abroad all mischievous principles, while the Church's claim to train and educate youth is in every way outraged and baffled. Such too is the purpose of the seizing of the temporal power, conferred many centuries ago by Divine Providence on the Bishop of Rome, that he might without let or hindrance use the authority conferred by Christ for the eternal welfare of the nations.

We have recalled to your minds, Venerable Brothers, this deathly mass of ills, not to increase the sorrow naturally caused you by this most sad state of things, but because we believe that from its consideration you will most plainly see how serious are the matters claiming our attention as well as devotedness, and with what energy we should work and, more than ever, under the present adverse conditions, protect, so far as in us lies, the Church of Christ and the honour of the Apostolic See —the objects of so many slanders—and assert their claims.

The Church is the mother of civil society. It is perfectly clear and evident, Venerable Brothers, that the very notion of civilization is a fiction of the brain, if it rest not on the abiding principles of truth and the unchanging laws of virtue and justice, and if unfeigned love knit not together the wills of men, and gently control the interchange and the character of their mutual service. Now, who would make bold to deny that the Church, by spreading the gospel throughout the nations, has brought the light of truth amongst people utterly savage and steeped in foul superstition, and has quickened them alike to recognize the Divine Author of nature and duly to respect themselves? Further, who will deny that the Church has done away with the curse of slavery and restored men to the original dignity of their noble nature; and—by uplifting the standard of Redemption in all quarters of the globe, by introducing, or shielding under her protection, the sciences and arts, by founding and taking into her keeping excellent charitable institutions which provide relief for ills of every kind—has throughout the world, in private or in public life, civilized the human race, freed it from degradation, and with all care trained it to a way of living such as befits the dignity and the hopes of man? And if any one of sound mind compare the age in which we live, so hostile to religion and to the Church of Christ, with those happy times when the Church was revered as a mother by the nations, beyond all question he will see that our epoch is rushing wildly along the straight road to destruction; while in those times which most abounded in excellent institutions, peaceful life, wealth and prosperity, the people showed themselves most obedient to the Church's rule and laws. Therefore, if the many blessings we have mentioned, due to the agency and saving help of the Church, are the true and worthy outcome of civilization, the Church of Christ, far from being alien to, or neglectful of progress, has a just claim to all men's praise as its nurse, its mistress, and its mother.

Civil society is vain or false if opposed to the Church's teaching and laws.

Furthermore, that kind of civilization which conflicts with the doctrines and laws of holy Church, is nothing but a worthless imitation and a meaningless name. Of this those peoples on whom the gospel light has never shone, afford ample proof, since in their mode of life a shadowy semblance only of civilization is discoverable, while its true and solid blessings have never been possessed. Undoubtedly that cannot by any means be accounted the perfection of civilized life which sets all legitimate authority boldly at defiance; nor can that be regarded as liberty which, shamefully and by the vilest means, spreading false principles, and freely indulging the sensual gratification of lustful desires, claims impunity for all crime and misdemeanour, and thwarts the goodly influence of the worthiest citizens of whatsoever class. Delusive, perverse and misleading, as are these principles, they cannot possibly have any inherent power to perfect the human race and fill it with blessing, for *sin maketh nations miserable*.* Such principles, as a matter of course, must hurry nations, corrupted in mind and heart, into every kind of infamy, weaken all right order, and thus, sooner or later, bring the standing and peace of the State to the very brink of ruin.

The Apostolic See has deserved well of all civil society.

Again, if we consider the achievements of the See of Rome, what can be more wicked than to deny

---

* *Prov.* xiv. 34.

how much and how well the Roman Bishops have served civilized society at large? For Our predecessors, to provide for the peoples' good, encountered struggles of every kind, endured to the utmost burdensome toils, and never hesitated to expose themselves to most dangerous trials. With eyes fixed on heaven, they neither bowed down their head before the threats of the wicked, nor allowed themselves to be led by flattery or bribes into unworthy compliance. This Apostolic Chair it was that gathered and held together the crumbling remains of the old order of things; this was the kindly light by whose help the culture of Christian times shone far and wide; this was an anchor of safety in the fierce storms by which the human race has been convulsed; this was the sacred bond of union that linked together nations distant in region and differing in character; in short, this was a common centre from which was sought instruction in faith and religion, no less than guidance and advice for the maintenance of peace and the functions of practical life. In very truth it is the glory of the supreme Pontiffs that they steadfastly set themselves up as a wall and a bulwark to save human society from falling back into its former superstition and barbarism.

Would that this healing authority had never been slighted or set aside! Assuredly neither would the civil power have lost that venerable and sacred glory, the lustrous gift of religion, which alone renders the state of subjection noble and worthy of man; nor would so many revolutions and wars have been fomented to ravage the world with desolation and bloodshed; nor would kingdoms, once so flourishing, but now fallen from the height of prosperity, lie crushed beneath the weight of every kind of calamity. Of this the peoples of the East also furnish an example, who, by breaking the most sweet yoke that bound them to this Apostolic See, forfeited the splendour of their former greatness, their renown in science and art, and the dignity of their sway.

The country of Italy has most of all experienced the Church's benefits.

Of these remarkable benefits, however, which illustrious monuments of all ages prove to have flowed upon every quarter of the world from the Apostolic See, this land of Italy has had the most abounding experience. For it has derived advantages from the See of Rome proportionate to the greater nearness of its natural situation. Unquestionably to the Roman Pontiffs it is that Italy must own herself indebted for the substantial glory and majesty by which she has been pre-eminent amongst nations. The influence and fatherly care of the Popes has upon many occasions shielded her from hostile attack and brought her relief and aid, the effect of which is that the Catholic faith has been ever maintained inviolate in the hearts of Italians.

These services of Our predecessors, to omit mention of many others, have been witnessed to in a special manner by the records of the times of St. Leo the Great, Alexander III., Innocent III., St. Pius V., Leo X. and other Pontiffs, by whose exertions or protection Italy has escaped unscathed from the utter destruction threatened by barbarians; has kept unimpaired her old faith, and, amid the darkness and defilement of a ruder age, has cultivated and preserved in vigour the lustre of science and the splendour of art. To this furthermore bears witness Our Own fostering City, the home of the Popes, which, under their rule, reaped this special benefit, that it not only was the strong citadel of the faith, but also became the refuge of the liberal arts and the very abode of culture, winning for itself the admiration and respect of the whole world. As these facts in all their amplitude have been handed down, in historical records, for the perpetual remembrance of posterity, it is easy to understand that it is only with hostile design and shameless calumny—meant to mislead men—that any one can venture in speech and in writing to accuse the Apostolic See of being an obstacle to the civil progress of nations and to the prosperity of Italy.

Seeing, therefore, that all the hopes of Italy and of the whole world lie in the power so beneficent to the common good and profit, wherewith the authority of the Apostolic See is endowed, and in the close union which binds all the faithful of Christ to the Roman Pontiff, We recognise that nothing should be nearer Our heart than how to preserve safe and sound the dignity of the Roman See, and to strengthen ever more and more the union of members with the Head, of the children with their Father.

Restoration of the Holy See to its former dignity and freedom.

Wherefore, that We may above all things, and in every possible way, maintain the rights and freedom of this Holy See, We shall never cease to strive that Our authority may meet with due deference; that obstacles may be removed which hamper the free exercise of Our ministry; and that We may be restored to that condition of things in which the design of God's wisdom had long ago placed the Roman Pontiffs. We are moved to demand this restoration, Venerable Brethren, not by any feeling of ambition or desire of supremacy, but by the nature of Our office and by Our sacred promise confirmed on oath ; and further, not only because this sovereignty is essential to protect and preserve the full liberty of the spiritual power, but also because it is an ascertained fact that, when the temporal sovereignty of the Apostolic See is in question, the cause of the public good and the well-being of all human society in general are also at stake. Hence We cannot omit, in the discharge of Our duty, which obliges us to guard the rights of Holy Church, to renew and confirm in every particular by this Our Letter those declarations and protests which Pius IX., of sacred memory, Our predecessor, on many and repeated occasions published against the seizing of the civil sovereignty and the infringement of rights belonging to the Roman Church. At the same time We address ourselves to Princes and chief rulers of the nations, and earnestly beseech them in the august name of the most High God, not to refuse the Church's aid, proffered them in a season of such need, but with united and friendly aims to join themselves to her as the source of authority and salvation, and to attach themselves to her more and more in the bonds of hearty love and devotedness. God grant that—seeing the truth of Our words and considering within themselves that the teaching of Christ is, as Augustine used to say, "a great blessing to the State, if obeyed,"*

---

* *Epistola* 138 (vel 5), ad Marcell. n. 15.

and that their own peace and safety, as well as that of their people, is bound up with the safety of the Church and the reverence due to her,—they may give their whole thought and care to mitigating the evils by which the Church and its visible Head are harassed, and so it may at last come to pass that the peoples whom they govern may enter on the way of justice and peace, and rejoice in a happy era of prosperity and glory.

<small>Union of the whole Catholic flock with the Supreme Pontiff in embracing truth and rejecting error.</small>

In the next place, in order that the union of hearts between their chief Pastor and the whole Catholic flock may daily be strengthened, We here call upon you, Venerable Brothers, with particular earnestness, and strongly urge you to kindle, with priestly zeal and pastoral care, the fire of the love of religion among the faithful entrusted to you, that their attachment to this chair of truth and justice may become closer and firmer, that they may welcome all its teachings with thorough assent of mind and will, wholly rejecting such opinions, even when most widely received, as they know to be contrary to the Church's doctrine. In this matter, the Roman Pontiffs, Our predecessors, and last of all, Pius IX. of sacred memory, especially in the General Council of the Vatican, have not neglected, so often as there was need, to condemn wide-spreading errors and to smite them with the Apostolic condemnation. This they did, keeping before their eyes the words of St. Paul : *Beware lest any man cheat you by philosophy and vain deceit, according to the tradition of men, according to the elements of the world and not according to Christ.* * All such censures, We, following

---

* 2 *Coloss.* ii. 8.

in the steps of Our predecessors, do confirm and renew from this Apostolic Seat of truth, whilst We earnestly ask of the Father of Lights that all the faithful, brought to thorough agreement in the like feeling and the same belief, may think and speak even as Ourselves. It is your duty, Venerable Brothers, sedulously to strive that the seed of heavenly doctrine be sown broadcast in the field of God, and that the teachings of the Catholic faith may be implanted early in the souls of the faithful, may strike deep root in them, and be kept free from the ruinous blight of error. The more the enemies of religion exert themselves to offer the uninformed, especially the young, such instruction as darkens the mind and corrupts morals, the more actively should we endeavour that not only a suitable and solid method of education may flourish, but above all that this education be wholly in harmony with the Catholic faith in its literature and system of training, and chiefly in philosophy, upon which the foundation of other sciences in great measure depends. Philosophy seeks not the overthrow of divine revelation, but delights rather to prepare its way, and defend it against assailants, both by example and in written works, as the great Augustine and the Angelic Doctor, with all other teachers of Christian wisdom, have proved to us.

Observance of God's law about matrimony and the family. Now the training of youth most conducive to the defence of true faith and religion and to the preservation of morality, must find its beginning from an early age within the circle of home life ; and this family Christian training, sadly undermined in these our times, cannot possibly be restored to its due dignity, save by those laws under which it was established in the Church by her Divine Founder Himself. Our Lord Jesus Christ, by raising to the dignity of a sacrament the contract of matrimony, in which He would have His Own union with the Church typified, not only made the marriage-tie more holy, but in addition provided efficacious sources of aid for parents and children alike, so that, by the discharge of their duties one to another, they might with greater ease attain to happiness both in time and in eternity. But when impious laws, setting at naught the sanctity of this great sacrament, put it on the same footing with mere civil contracts, the lamentable result followed, that, outraging the dignity of Christian matrimony, citizens made use of legalised concubinage in place of marriage; husband and wife neglected their bounden duty to each other; children refused obedience and reverence to their parents; the bonds of domestic love were loosened; and, alas! the worst scandal and of all the most ruinous to public morality, very frequently an unholy passion opened the door to disastrous and fatal separations. These most unhappy and painful consequences, Venerable Brothers, cannot fail to arouse your zeal, and move you constantly and earnestly to warn the faithful committed to your charge, to listen with docility to your teaching regarding the holiness of Christian marriage, and to obey the laws by which the Church controls the duties of married people and of their offspring.

Then, indeed, will that most desirable result come about, that the character and conduct of individuals also will be reformed; for just as from a rotten stock are produced healthless branches or worthless fruits, so do the ravages of a pestilence which ruins the household spread wide their cruel infection to the hurt and injury of individual citizens. On the other hand, when domestic society is fashioned in the mould of Christian life, each member will gradually grow accustomed to the love of religion and piety, to the abhorrence of false and harmful teaching, to the pursuit of virtue, to obedience to elders, and to the restraint of that insatiable seeking after self interest alone, which so spoils and weakens the character of men. To this end it will certainly help not a little to encourage and promote those pious Associations which have been established, in our own times especially, with so great profit to the cause of the Catholic religion.

Great indeed and beyond the strength of man are these objects of our hopes and prayers, Venerable Brothers; but since God has *made the nations of the earth for health,* * when He founded the Church for the welfare of the peoples, and promised that He will abide with her by His assistance to the end of the world, We firmly trust that, through your endeavours, the human race, taking warning from so many evils and visitations, will submit themselves at length to the Church, and turn for health and prosperity to the infallible guidance of this Apostolic See.

Rejoicing on account of union of hearts and minds. Meanwhile, Venerable Brothers, before bringing this Letter to a close, We must express Our congratulations on the striking harmony and concord which unites your minds among yourselves and with this Apostolic

---

* *Wisdom* i. 14.

See. This perfect union We regard as not merely an impregnable bulwark against hostile attacks, but also as an auspicious and happy omen, presaging better times for the Church; and, while it yields great relief to Our weakness, it seasonably encourages Us to endure with readiness all labours and all struggles on behalf of God's Church in the arduous task which We have undertaken.

Thanks for tokens of obedience received. Moreover, from the causes of hope and rejoicing which We have made known to you, We cannot separate those tokens of love and obedience, which you, Venerable Brethren, in these first days of Our Pontificate, have shown Our lowliness, and with you so many of the clergy and the faithful, who, by letters sent, by offerings given, by pilgrimages undertaken, and by other works of love, have made it clear that the devotion and charity which they manifested to Our most worthy predecessor, still lasts, so strong and steadfast and unchanged, as not to slacken towards the person of a successor so much inferior. For these splendid tokens of Catholic piety We humbly confess to the Lord that He is good and gracious, while to you, Venerable Brothers, and to all Our beloved children from whom We have received them, We publicly, from the bottom of Our heart, avow the grateful feelings of Our soul, cherishing the fullest confidence that, in the present critical state of things and in the difficulties of the times, this your devotion and love and the devotion and love of the faithful will never fail Us. Nor have We any doubt that these conspicuous examples of filial piety and Christian virtue will be of such avail as to make our most merciful

God, moved by these dutiful deeds, look with favour on His flock and grant the Church peace and victory. But as We are sure that this peace and victory will more quickly and more readily be given Us, if the faithful are unremitting in their prayers and supplications to obtain it, We earnestly exhort you, Venerable Brothers, to stir up for this end the zeal and ardour of the faithful, taking the Immaculate Queen of Heaven as their intercessor with God, and having recourse as their advocates to St. Joseph, the heavenly Patron of the Church, and to SS. Peter and Paul, the Princes of the Apostles. To the powerful patronage of all these We humbly commit Our lowliness, all ranks of the ecclesiastical hierarchy, and all the flock of Christ our Lord.

For the rest, We trust that these days, on which We renew the memory of Jesus Christ, risen from the dead, may be to you, Venerable Brothers, and to all the fold of God a source of blessing and salvation and fulness of holy joy, praying our most gracious God that by the Blood of the Lamb without spot, which blotted out the handwriting that was against us, the sins we have committed may be washed away, and the judgment we are suffering for them may mercifully be mitigated.

The grace, of our Lord Jesus Christ, and the charity of God, and the communication of the Holy Ghost be with you all,* Venerable Brothers; to each and all of whom, as well as to Our beloved children, the clergy and faithful of your churches, as a pledge of Our special goodwill and as an earnest of the protection of heaven, We lovingly impart the Apostolic Benediction.

---

* 2 *Cor.* xii. 13.

THE CHRISTIAN CONSTITUTION OF STATES.

(Encyclical Letter, November 1, 1885.)

The Church is the nursing mother of civilization.

THE CATHOLIC CHURCH, that imperishable handiwork of our all-merciful God, has for her immediate and natural purpose the saving of souls and securing our happiness in heaven. Yet in regard to things temporal she is the source of benefits as manifold and great as if the chief end of her existence were to ensure the prospering of our earthly life. And in truth, wherever the Church has set her foot, she has straightway changed the face of things, and has attempered the moral tone of the people with a new civilization, and with virtues before unknown. All nations which have yielded to her sway have become eminent for their culture, their sense of justice, and the glory of their high deeds.

Yet she has been traduced from the beginning as an enemy of progress and prosperity in the civil order.

And yet a hackneyed reproach of old date is levelled against her, that the Church is opposed to the rightful aims of the civil government, and is wholly unable to afford help in spreading that welfare and progress which justly and naturally are sought after by every well regulated State. From the very beginning Christians were harassed by slanderous accusations of this nature, and on that account

E

were held up to hatred and execration, for being (so they were called) enemies of the empire. The Christian religion was moreover commonly charged with being the cause of the calamities that so frequently befell the state, whereas, in very truth, just punishment was being awarded to guilty nations by an avenging God. This odious calumny, with most valid reason, nerved the genius and sharpened the pen of St. Augustine, who, notably in his treatise *On the City of God*, set forth in so bright a light the worth of Christian wisdom in its relation to the public weal, that he seems not merely to have pleaded the cause of the Christians of his day, but to have refuted for all future times impeachments so grossly contrary to truth.

An opinion favoured by many nowadays traces the origin of the maxims of social morality to other sources than the teaching of the Church.

The wicked proneness, however, to levy the like charges and accusations has not been lulled to rest. Many, indeed, are they who have tried to work out a plan of civil society based on doctrines other than those approved by the Catholic Church. Nay, in these latter days a novel scheme of law has begun here and there to gain increase and influence, the outcome, as it is maintained, of an age arrived at full stature, and the result of liberty in evolution. But though endeavours of various kinds have been ventured on, it is clear that no better mode has been devised for the building up and ruling the State than that which is the necessary growth of the teachings of the Gospel. We deem it, therefore, of the highest moment, and a strict duty of Our Apostolic office, to contrast with the lessons taught by Christ the novel theories now advanced

THE CHRISTIAN CONSTITUTION OF STATES. 67

The modern system of state polity compared with the Christian jurisprudence.

touching the State. By this means We cherish hope that the bright shining of the truth may scatter the mists of error and doubt, so that one and all may see clearly the imperious law of life which they are bound to follow and obey.

It is not difficult to determine what would be the form and character of the State were it governed according to the principles of Christian philosophy. Man's natural instinct moves him to live in civil society, for he cannot, if dwelling apart, provide himself with the necessary requirements of life, nor procure the means of developing his mental and moral faculties. Hence it is divinely ordained that he should lead his life—be it family, social, or civil,—with his fellow-men, amongst whom alone his several wants can be adequately supplied. But as no society can hold together unless some one be over all, directing all to strive earnestly for the common good, every civilized community must have a ruling authority, and this authority, no less than society itself, has its source in nature, and has, consequently, God for its author. Hence it follows that all public power must proceed from God. For God alone is the true and supreme Lord of the world. Everything, without exception, must be subject to Him, and must serve Him, so that whosoever holds the right to govern, holds it

Civil society is founded by God, the Author of Nature.

Hence God is the source of public authority, and of the right to rule.

In order to a just and paternal exercise of authority the sovereign power must take pattern from God.

from one sole and single source, namely God, the Sovereign Ruler of all. *There is no power but from God.**

The right to rule is not necessarily, however, bound up with any special mode of government. It may take this or that form, provided only that it be of a nature to insure the general welfare. But whatever be the nature of the government, rulers must ever bear in mind that God is the paramount Ruler of the world, and must set Him before themselves as their exemplar and law in the administration of the State. For, in things visible, God has fashioned secondary causes, in which His Divine action can in some wise be discerned, leading up to the end to which the course of the world is ever tending. In like manner in Civil society, God has always willed that there should be a ruling authority, and that they who are invested with it should reflect the Divine power and providence in some measure over the human race.

They, therefore, who rule should rule with even-handed justice, not as masters, but rather as fathers, for the rule of God over man is most just, and is tempered always with a father's kindness. Government should moreover be administered for the well-being of the citizens, because they who govern others possess authority solely for the welfare of the State. Furthermore, the Civil power must not be subservient to the advantage of any one individual, or of some few persons; inasmuch as it was established for the common good of all. But if those who are in authority rule unjustly, if they

---

* *Rom.* xiii. 1.

govern overbearingly or arrogantly, and if their measures prove hurtful to the people, they must remember that the Almighty will one day bring them to account, the more strictly in proportion to the sacredness of their office and pre-eminence of their dignity. *The mighty shall be mightily tormented.** Then truly will the majesty of the law meet with the dutiful and willing homage of the people, when they are convinced that their rulers hold authority from God, and feel that it is a matter of justice and duty to obey them, and to show them reverence and fealty, united to a love not unlike that which children show their parents. *Let every soul be subject to higher powers.* † To despise legitimate authority, in whomsoever vested, is unlawful, as a rebellion against the Divine will, and whoever resists that, rushes wilfully to destruction. *He that resisteth the power resisteth the ordinance of God, and they that resist, purchase to themselves damnation.* ‡ To cast aside obedience, and by popular violence to incite to revolt, is therefore treason, not against man only, but against God.

The obedience of subjects, for God's sake, is honourable and holy.

Society, being a moral person, is bound to pay due homage to God. As a consequence, the State, constituted as it is, is clearly bound to act up to the manifold and weighty duties linking it to God, by the public profession of religion. Nature and reason, which command every individual devoutly to worship God in holiness, because we belong to Him and must return to Him since from Him we came, bind also the civil community by a like law. For men living

---

* *Wisd.* vi. 7.   † *Rom.* xiii. 1.   ‡ *Rom.* xiii. 2.

together in society are under the power of God no less than individuals are, and society, not less than individuals, owes gratitude to God, Who gave it being and maintains it, and Whose ever-bounteous goodness enriches it with countless blessings. Since, then, no one is allowed to be remiss in the service due to God, and since the chief duty of all men is to cling to religion in both its teaching and practice—not such religion as they may have a preference for, but the religion which God enjoins, and which certain and most clear marks show to be the only one true religion,—it is a public crime to act as though there were no God. So too is it a sin in the State not to have care for religion, as a something beyond its scope, or as of no practical benefit; or out of many forms of religion to adopt that one which chimes in with the fancy; for we are bound absolutely to worship God in that way which He has shown to be His will. All who rule, therefore, should hold in honour the holy Name of God, and one of their chief duties must be to favour religion, to protect it, to shield it under the credit and sanction of the laws, and neither to organise nor enact any measure that may compromise its safety. This is the bounden duty of rulers to the people over whom they rule. For one and all are we destined, by our birth and adoption, to enjoy, when this frail and fleeting life is ended, a supreme and final good in heaven, and to the attainment of this every endeavour should be directed. Since then upon this depends the full and perfect happiness of mankind, the securing of this end should be of all imaginable interests the most urgent. Hence Civil society, established for the common welfare, should not only safeguard the well-being of the community, but have also at heart the interests of its individual members, in such mode as not in any way to hinder, but in every manner to render as easy as may be, the possession of that highest and unchangeable good for which all should seek. Wherefore, for this purpose, care must especially be taken to preserve unharmed and unimpeded the religion whereof the practice is the link connecting man with his God.

Society is bound, as a consequence, to help its members to attain their last end.

Now it cannot be difficult to find out which is the true Religion, if only it be sought with an earnest and unbiassed mind; for proofs are abundant and striking. We have, for example, the fulfilment of prophecies; miracles in great number; the rapid spread of the faith in the midst of enemies and in face of overwhelming obstacles; the witness of the martyrs, and the like. From all these it is evident that the only true religion is the one established by Jesus Christ Himself, and which He committed to His Church to protect and to propagate.

Ecclesiastical society, which is the Church, is instituted by Christ,

For the only-begotten Son of God established on earth a Society which is called the Church, and to it He handed over the exalted and divine office which He had received from His Father, to be continued through the ages to come. *As the Father hath sent Me, I also send you.* *

with a view to the everlasting salvation of souls.

Behold I am with you, all days, even to the consummation of the

---

* *John* xx. 21.

world. * Consequently, as Jesus Christ came into the world that men *might have life and have it more abundantly,* † so also has the Church for its aim and end the eternal salvation of souls, and hence it is so constituted as to open wide its arms to all mankind, unhampered by any limit of either time or place. *Preach ye the Gospel to every creature.* ‡

The Church is a universal society, Over this mighty multitude God has Himself set rulers with power to govern; and He has willed that one should be the head of all, and the chief and unerring teacher of truth, to whom **with a distinction of grades and offices,** He has given *the keys of the kingdom of heaven.* ‖ *Feed My lambs, feed My sheep.* § *I have prayed for thee that thy faith fail not.* ¶

This Society is made up of men, **both natural and supernatural,** just as Civil society is, and yet is supernatural and spiritual, on account of the end for which it was founded, and of the means by which it aims at attaining that end. Hence it is distinguished, and differs, from civil society, and what is of highest moment, it is a society chartered as of right divine, perfect in its nature and in its title, to possess in itself and by itself, through the will and loving kindness of its Founder, all **complete, independent, and supreme,** needful provision for its maintenance and action. And just as the end at which the Church aims is by far the noblest of ends, so is its authority the most exalted of all authority,

---

* *Matthew* xxviii. 20.   † *John* x. 10.   ‡ *Mark* xvi. 15.
‖ *Matt.* xvi. 19.   § *John* xxi. 16-17.   ¶ *Luke* xxii. 32.

nor can it be looked upon as inferior to the Civil power, or in any manner dependent upon it.

In very truth Jesus Christ gave to His Apostles unrestrained authority in regard to things sacred, together with the genuine and most true power of making laws, as also with the two-fold right of judging and of punishing, which flow from that power. *All power is given to Me in heaven and on earth: going therefore teach all nations... teaching them to observe whatever I have commanded you.* * And in another place, *If he will not hear them, tell the Church.*† And again, *In readiness to revenge all disobedience.*‡ And once more, *That ... I may not deal more severely according to the power which the Lord hath given me, unto edification and not unto destruction.*|| Hence it is the Church, and not the State, that is to be man's guide to heaven. It is to the Church that God has assigned the charge of seeing to, and legislating for, all that concerns religion; of teaching all nations; of spreading the Christian faith as widely as possible; in short, of administering all her affairs freely and without hindrance, in accordance with her own judgment, all matters that fall within its competence.

<small>Invested with legislative and judicial power.</small>

Now this authority, perfect in itself, and plainly meant to be unfettered, so long assailed by a philosophy that truckles to the State, the Church has never ceased to claim for herself, and openly to exercise. The Apostles themselves were the first to uphold it, when, being forbidden by the rulers of the Synagogue to preach the Gospel,

---

* *Matthew* xxviii. 18, 19, 20. † *Ibid.* xviii. 17. ‡ 2 *Cor.* x. 6.
|| *Ibid.* xiii. 10.

This authority is complete and self-dependent. they courageously answered, *We must obey God rather than men.** This same authority the holy Fathers of the Church were always careful to maintain by weighty arguments, according as occasion arose, and the Roman Pontiffs have never shrunk from defending it with unbending constancy. Nay more, princes and all invested with power to rule have themselves approved it, in theory alike and in practice. It cannot be called in question that in the making of treaties, in the transaction of business matters, in the sending and receiving ambassadors, and in the interchange of other kinds of official dealings, they have been wont to treat with the Church as with a supreme and legitimate power. And assuredly all ought to hold that it was not without a singular disposition of God's providence, that this power of the Church was provided with a civil sovereignty as the surest safeguard of her independence.

The two-fold authority, that of the Church and that of the Civil government, established by God. The Almighty, therefore, has appointed the charge of the human race between two powers, the Ecclesiastical and the Civil, the one being set over divine, and the other over human, things. Each in its kind is supreme, each has fixed limits within which it is contained, limits which are defined by the nature and special object of the province of each, so that there is, we may say, an orbit traced out within which the action of each is brought into play by its own native right. But inasmuch as each of

---

* *Acts* v. 29.

these two powers has authority over the same subjects, and as it might come to pass that one and the same thing—related differently, but still remaining one and the same thing—might belong to the jurisdiction and determination of both, therefore God, Who foresees all things, and Who is the Author of these two powers, has marked out the course of each in right correlation to the other. *For the powers that are, are ordained of God.** Were this not so, deplorable contentions and conflicts would often arise, and not unfrequently men, like travellers at the meeting of two roads, would hesitate in anxiety and doubt, not knowing what course to follow. Two powers would be commanding contrary things, and it would be a dereliction of duty to disobey either of the two.

<small>Both of which are confined within certain limits.</small>

But it would be most repugnant to deem thus of the wisdom and goodness of God. Even in physical things, albeit of a lower order, the Almighty has so combined the forces and springs of nature with tempered action and wondrous harmony, that no one of them clashes with any other, and all of them most fitly and aptly work together for the great purpose of the universe. There must, accordingly, exist, between these two powers, a certain orderly connection, which may be compared to the union of the soul and body in man. The nature and scope of that connection, can be determined only, as We have laid down, by having regard to the nature of each power, and by taking

<small>Between these two powers there exists a certain orderly connection.</small>

---

* *Rom.* viii. 1.

account of the relative excellence and nobleness of their purpose. One of the two has for its proximate and chief object the well-being of this mortal life; the other the everlasting joys of heaven. Whatever, therefore,

Sacred things are subject to the authority of the Church.

in things human is of a sacred character, whatever belongs either of its own nature or by reason of the end to which it is referred, to the salvation of souls, or to the worship of God, is subject to the power and judgment of the Church. Whatever is to be ranged under the civil and political order is rightly subject to the Civil authority. Jesus Christ has Himself given command that what is Cæsar's is to be rendered to Cæsar, and that what belongs to God is to be rendered to God.

Concordats.

There are, nevertheless, occasions when another method of concord is available, for the sake of peace and liberty: We mean when rulers of the State and the Roman Pontiff come to an understanding touching some special matter. At such times the Church gives signal proof of her motherly love by showing the greatest possible kindliness and indulgence.

Such then, as We have briefly pointed out, is the Christian organisation of Civil society: not rashly or fancifully shaped out, but educed from the highest and truest principles, confirmed by natural reason itself.

The Christian idea of Civil Polity is unexceptionable.

In such an organization of the State, there is nothing that can be thought to infringe upon the dignity of rulers, and nothing unbecoming them; nay, so far from degrading the Sovereign power in its due rights, it adds to it permanence and lustre. Indeed, when more fully pondered, this mutual co-ordination has a perfection in which all other forms of government are lacking, and from which excellent results would flow, were the several component parts to keep their place, and duly discharge the office and work appointed respectively for each. And, doubtless, in the Constitution of the State such as we have described, divine and human things are equitably shared; the rights of citizens assured to them, and fenced round by divine, by natural, and by human law; the duties incumbent on each one being wisely marked out, and their fulfilment fittingly ensured. In their uncertain and toilsome journey towards *the city made without hands*, all see that they have safe guides and helpers on their way, and are conscious that others have charge to protect their persons alike and their possessions, and to obtain or preserve for them everything essential for their present life. Furthermore, domestic society acquires that firmness and solidity so needful to it, from the holiness of marriage, one and indissoluble, wherein the rights and duties of husband and wife are controlled with wise justice and equity; due honour is assured to the woman; the authority of the husband is conformed to the pattern afforded by the authority of God; the power of the father is tempered by a due regard for the dignity of the mother and her offspring; and the best possible provision is made for the guardianship, welfare, and education of the children.

Advantages to be derived from the Christian Civil Polity,

In both the family and society at large.

In political affairs, and all matters civil, the laws aim

at securing the common good, and are not framed according to the delusive caprices and opinions of the mass of the people, but by truth and by justice; the ruling powers are invested with a sacredness more than human, and are withheld from deviating from the path of duty, and from overstepping the bounds of rightful authority; and the obedience of citizens is rendered with a feeling of honour and dignity, since obedience is not the servitude of man to man, but submission to the will of God, exercising His sovereignty through the medium of men. Now, this being recognised as undeniable, it is felt that the high office of rulers should be held in respect; that public authority should be constantly and faithfully obeyed; that no act of sedition should be committed; and that the civic order of the commonwealth should be maintained as sacred.

<small>and in benefit of the social order.</small>

So, also, as to the duties of each one towards his fellow-men, mutual forbearance, kindliness, generosity, are placed in the ascendant; the man who is at once a citizen and a Christian is not drawn aside by conflicting obligations; and, lastly, the abundant benefits with which the Christian religion, of its very nature, endows even the mortal life of man, are acquired for the community and civil society. And this to such an extent that it may be said in sober truth: "The condition of the commonwealth depends on the religion with which God is worshipped: and between one and the other there exists an intimate and abiding connection."*

---

* *Sacr. Imp. ad Cyrillum Alexand. et Episcopos Metrop.* Cfr. Labbe, *Collect. Conc.*, *T.* iii.

Admirably, according to his wont, does St. Augustine, in many passages, enlarge upon the potency of these advantages; but nowhere more markedly and to the point than when he addresses the Catholic Church in the following words: "Thou dost teach and train children with much tenderness, young men with much vigour, old men with much gentleness; as the age not of the body alone, but of the mind of each requires. Women thou dost subject to their husbands in chaste and faithful obedience, not for the gratifying of their lust, but for bringing forth children, and for having a share in the family concerns. Thou dost set husbands over their wives, not that they may play false to the weaker sex, but according to the requirements of sincere affection. Thou dost subject children to their parents in a kind of free service, and dost establish parents over their children with a benign rule. . . . Thou joinest together, not in society only, but in a sort of brotherhood, citizen with citizen, nation with nation, and the whole race of men, by reminding them of their common parentage. Thou teachest kings to look to the interests of their people, and dost admonish the people to be submissive to their kings. With all care dost thou teach all to whom honour is due, and affection, and reverence, and fear, consolation, and admonition, and exhortation, and discipline, and reproach, and punishment. Thou showest that all these are not equally incumbent on all, but that charity is owing to all, and wrong-doing to none." * And in another place, blaming the false wisdom

St. Augustine enlarges admirably on these benefits.

---

* *De moribus Eccl. Cathol.*, xxx. 63.

of certain time-serving philosophers, he observes: "Let those who say that the teaching of Christ is hurtful to the State, produce such armies as the maxims of Jesus have enjoined soldiers to bring into being; such governors of provinces; such husbands and wives; such parents and children; such masters and servants; such kings; such judges, and such payers and collectors of tribute, as the Christian teaching instructs them to become, and then let them dare to say that such teaching is hurtful to the State. Nay, rather, will they not hesitate to own that this discipline, if duly acted up to, is the very mainstay of the commonwealth?" *

There was once a time when States were governed by the principles of Gospel teaching. Then it was that the power and divine virtue of Christian wisdom had diffused itself throughout the laws, institutions and morals of the people; permeating all ranks and relations of Civil society. Then too, the religion instituted by Jesus Christ, established firmly in befitting dignity, flourished everywhere, by the favour of princes and the legitimate protection of magistrates; and Church and State were happily united in concord and friendly interchange of good offices. The State constituted in this wise, bore fruits important beyond all expectation, whose remembrance is still, and always will be, in renown, witnessed to as they are by countless proofs which can never be blotted out or even obscured by any craft of any enemies. Christian Europe has subdued barbarous nations, and changed

History witnesses to these advantages.

---

* *Epist. 138, al. 5, ad Marcellinum*, ii. 15.

them from a savage to a civilized condition, from superstition to true worship. It victoriously rolled back the tide of Mohammedan conquest; retained the headship of civilization; stood forth in the front rank as the leader and teacher of all, in every branch of national culture; bestowed on the world the gift of true and many-sided liberty; and most wisely founded very numerous institutions for the solace of human suffering. And if we inquire how it was able to bring about so altered a condition of things, the answer is—Beyond all question, in large measure, through Religion; under whose auspices so many great undertakings were set on foot, through whose aid they were brought to completion.

A similar state of things would certainly have continued had the agreement of the two powers been lasting. More important results even might have been justly looked for, had obedience waited upon the authority, teaching, and counsels of the Church, and had this submission been specially marked by greater and more unswerving loyalty. For that should be regarded in the light of an ever-changeless law which Ivo of Chartres wrote to Pope Paschal II.: " When kingdom and priesthood are at one, in complete accord, the world is well ruled, and the Church flourishes, and brings forth abundant fruit. But when they are at variance, not only smaller interests prosper not, but even things of greatest moment fall into deplorable decay." *

---

* *Epist.* 238.

The new jurisprudence traced to the revolution of the xvi. century.

Sad it is to call to mind how the harmful and lamentable rage for innovation which rose to a climax in the sixteenth century, threw first of all into confusion the Christian religion, and next, by natural sequence, invaded the precincts of philosophy, whence it spread amongst all classes of society. From this source, as from a fountain-head, burst forth all those later tenets of unbridled license which, in the midst of the terrible upheavals of the last century, were wildly conceived and boldly proclaimed as the principles and foundation of that *new jurisprudence* which was not merely previously unknown, but was at variance on many points with not only the Christian, but even with the natural law.

The main principle being the false claim of absolute equality of all men.

Amongst these principles the main one lays down that as all men are alike by race and nature, so in like manner all are equal in the control of their life; that each one is so far his own master as to be in no sense under the rule of any other individual; that each is free to think on every subject just as he may choose, and to do whatever he may like to do; that no man has any right to rule over other men. In a society grounded upon such maxims, all government is nothing more nor less than the will of the people, and the people, being under the power of itself alone, is alone its own ruler. It does choose nevertheless some to whose charge it may commit itself, but in such wise that it makes over to them not the right so much as the business of governing, to be exercised however in its name.

THE CHRISTIAN CONSTITUTION OF STATES. 83

Whence it follows that the will of the people is looked upon as the sole law. The authority of God is passed over in silence, just as if there were no God; or as if He cared nothing for human society; or as if men whether in their individual capacity or bound together in social relations, owed nothing to God; or as if there could be a government of which the whole origin and power and authority did not reside in God Himself. Thus, as is evident, a State becomes nothing but a multitude, which is its own master and ruler. And since the populace is declared to contain within itself the spring-head of all rights and of all power, it follows that the State does not consider itself bound by any kind of duty towards God. Moreover, it believes that it is not obliged to make public profession of any religion; or to **Religious indifference throughout society is openly maintained;** inquire which of the very many religions is the only one true; or to prefer one religion to all the rest; or to show to any form of religion special favour; but on the contrary is bound to grant equal rights to every creed, so that public order may not be disturbed by any particular form of religious belief.

And it is a part of this theory that all questions that concern religion are to be referred to private judgment; that every one is to be free to follow whatever religion he prefers, or none at all if he disapprove of all. **also the so-called liberty of Conscience.** From this the following consequences logically flow : that the judgment of each one's conscience is independent of all law; that the most unrestrained opinions may be openly expressed as to the practice or omission of Divine

Worship; and that every one has unbounded license to think whatever he chooses and to publish abroad whatever he thinks.

Those who adopt these maxims deny that the Church is a complete society; Now when the State rests on foundations like those just named —and for the time being they are greatly in favour,—it readily appears into what and how unrightful a position the Church is driven. For when the management of public business is in harmony with doctrines of such a kind, the Catholic religion is allowed a standing in Civil society equal only, or inferior, to societies alien from it; no regard is paid to the laws of the Church, and she who, by the order and commission of Jesus Christ, has the duty of teaching all nations, finds herself forbidden to take any part in the instruction of the people. With reference to matters that are of twofold jurisdiction, they who administer the Civil power lay down the law at their own will, and in matters that appertain to religion, defiantly put aside the most sacred decrees of the Church. They claim jurisdiction over **and seek to sever the affairs of the Church from those of the State.** the marriages of Catholics, even over the bond as well as the unity and the indissolubility of matrimony. They lay hands on the goods of the clergy, contending that the Church cannot possess property. Lastly, they treat the Church with such arrogance that, rejecting entirely her title to the nature and rights of a perfect Society, they hold that she differs in no respect from other societies in the State, and for this reason possesses no right nor any legal power of action, save that which she holds by the concession and favour of the government. If in any State the Church retains her own right—and this with the approval of the Civil law, owing to an agreement publicly entered into by the two powers—men forthwith begin to cry out that matters affecting the Church must be separated from those of the State.

Their object in uttering this cry is to be able to violate unpunished their plighted faith, and in all things to have unchecked control. And as the Church, unable to abandon her chiefest and most sacred duties, cannot patiently put up with this, and asks that the pledge given to her be fully and scrupulously acted up to, contentions frequently arise between the Ecclesiastical and the Civil power, of which the issue commonly is, that the weaker power yields to the one which is stronger in human resources.

<small>Proofs that this system is at variance with the teachings of reason.</small> Accordingly, it has become the practice and determination under this condition of public polity (now so much admired by many) either to forbid the action of the Church altogether, or to keep her in check and bondage to the State. Public enactments are in great measure framed with this design. The drawing up of laws, the administration of State affairs, the godless education of youth, the spoliation and suppression of Religious Orders, the overthrow of the Temporal Power of the Roman Pontiff, all alike aim at this one end—to paralyze the action of Christian institutions, to cramp to the utmost the freedom of the Catholic Church, and to curtail her every single prerogative.

Now, natural reason itself proves convincingly that

such concepts of the government of a State are wholly at variance with the truth. Nature itself bears witness that all power, of every kind, has its origin from God, Who is its chief and most august Source.

The sovereignty of the people, however, and this without any reference to God, is held to reside in the multitude; which is doubtless a doctrine exceedingly well calculated to flatter and to inflame many passions, but which lacks all reasonable proof, and all power of insuring public safety and preserving order. Indeed from the prevalence of this teaching, things have come to such a pass that many hold as an axiom of civil jurisprudence that seditions may be rightfully fostered. For the opinion prevails that princes are nothing more than delegates chosen to carry out the will of the people; whence it necessarily follows that all things are as changeable as the will of the people, so that risk of public disturbance is ever hanging over our heads.

Religious indifference. To hold therefore that there is no difference in matters of religion between forms that are unlike each other, and even contrary to each other, most clearly leads in the end to the rejection of all religion in both theory and practice. And this is the same thing as atheism, however it may differ from it in name. Men who really believe in the existence of God must, in order to be consistent with themselves and to avoid absurd conclusions, understand that differing modes of Divine Worship involving dissimilarity and conflict even on most important points, cannot all be equally probable, equally good, and equally acceptable to God.

The liberty of the Press. So, too, the liberty of thinking, and of publishing, whatsoever each one likes, without any hindrance, is not in itself an advantage over which society can wisely rejoice. On the contrary, it is the fountain-head and origin of many evils. Liberty is a power perfecting man, and hence should have truth and goodness for its object. But the character of goodness and truth cannot be changed at option. These remain ever one and the same, and are no less unchangeable than Nature herself. If the mind assents to false opinions, and the will chooses and follows after what is wrong, neither can attain its native fulness, but both must fall from their native dignity into an abyss of corruption. Whatever, therefore, is opposed to virtue and truth, may not rightly be brought temptingly before the eye of man, much less sanctioned by the favour and protection of the law. A well-spent life is the only passport to heaven, whither all are bound, and on this account the State is acting against the laws and dictates of nature whenever it permits the license of opinion and of action to lead minds astray from truth, and souls away from the practice of virtue. To exclude the

Exclusion of the Church from the business of life, from the school, and from the family. Church, founded by God Himself, from the business of life, from the power of making laws, from the training of youth, from domestic society, is a grave and fatal error. A State from which religion is banished can never be well regulated; and already perhaps more than is desirable is known of the nature and tendency of the so-called *civil* philosophy of life and morals. The Church of Christ is the true and sole teacher of virtue and guardian of morals. She it is who preserves in their purity the principles from which duties flow, and by setting forth most urgent reasons for virtuous life, bids us not only to turn away from wicked deeds, but even to curb all movements of the mind that are opposed to reason; even though they be not carried out in action.

The Church enslaved by the Civil Power.

To wish the Church to be subject to the Civil Power in the exercise of her duty is a great folly and a sheer injustice. Whenever this is the case, order is disturbed, for things natural are put above things supernatural; the many benefits which the Church, if free to act, would confer on society are either prevented or at least lessened in number; and a way is prepared for enmities and contentions between the two powers; with how evil result to both the issue of events has taught us only too frequently.

Condemnation of these erroneous tenets by the Supreme Pontiffs.

Doctrines such as these, which cannot be approved by human reason, and most seriously affect the whole Civil order, Our predecessors the Roman Pontiffs (well aware of what their Apostolic office required of them) have never allowed to pass uncondemned. Thus Gregory XVI. in his Encyclical Letter *Mirari vos*, of date August 15th, 1832, inveighed with weighty words against the sophisms, which even at his time were being publicly inculcated—namely, that no preference should be shown for any particular form of worship; that it is right for individuals to form their own personal judgments about religion; that each man's conscience is his sole and all-sufficing guide; and that it is lawful for every man to publish his own views, whatever they may be, and even to conspire against the State. On the question of the separation of Church and State the same Pontiff writes as follows : " Nor can we hope for happier results either for Religion or for the Civil Government from the wishes of those who desire that the Church be separated from the State, and the concord between the secular and ecclesiastical authority be dissolved. It is clear that these men, who yearn for a shameless liberty, live in dread of an agreement which has always been fraught with good, and advantageous alike to sacred and civil interests." To the like effect, also, as occasion presented itself, did Pius IX. brand publicly many false opinions which were gaining ground, and afterwards ordered them to be condensed in summary form in order that in this sea of error Catholics might have a light which they might safely follow.*

---

* It will suffice to indicate a few of them :

Prop. xix. The Church is not a true, perfect, and wholly independent society, possessing its own unchanging rights conferred upon it by its Divine Founder; but it is for the Civil power to determine what are the rights of the Church, and the limits within which it may use them.

Prop. xxxix. The State, as the origin and source of all rights, enjoys a right that is unlimited.

Prop. lv. The Church must be separated from the State, and the State from the Church.

Prop. lxxix. . . . It is untrue that the Civil liberty of every form of worship, and the full power given to all of openly and publicly manifesting whatsoever opinions and thoughts, lead to the more ready corruption of the minds and morals of the people, and to the spread of the plague of religious indifference.

The true import of these Papal utterances.

From these pronouncements of the Popes it is evident that the origin of public power is to be sought for in God Himself, and not in the multitude, and that it is repugnant to reason to allow free scope for sedition. Again, that it is not lawful for the State, any more than for the individual, either to disregard all religious duties, or to hold in equal favour different kinds of religion; that the unrestrained freedom of thinking and of openly making known one's thoughts is not inherent in the rights of citizens, and is by no means to be reckoned worthy of favour and support. In like manner it is to be understood that the Church no less than the State itself is a Society perfect in its own nature and its own right, and that those who exercise sovereignty ought not so to act as to compel the Church to become subservient or subject to them, or to hamper her liberty in the management of her own affairs, or to despoil her in any way of the other privileges conferred upon her by Jesus Christ. In matters, however, of mixed jurisdiction, it is in the highest degree consonant to nature, as also to the designs of God, that so far from one of the powers separating itself from the other, or still less coming into conflict with it, complete harmony, such as is suited to the end for which each power exists, should be preserved between them.

Rejection of distorted meanings assigned to them.

This then is the teaching of the Catholic Church concerning the Constitution and government of the State. By the words and decrees just cited, if judged dispassionately, no one of the several forms of government

THE CHRISTIAN CONSTITUTION OF STATES. 91

For instance the Popes in no wise proscribe any form of government;
is in itself condemned, inasmuch as none of them contain anything contrary to Catholic doctrine, and all of them are capable, if wisely and justly managed, to insure the welfare of the State. Neither is it blameworthy in itself, in any manner, for the people to have a share, greater or less, in the government: for at certain times, and under certain laws, such participation may not only be of benefit to the citizens, but may even be of obligation. Nor is there any reason why any one should accuse the Church of being wanting in gentleness of action or largeness of view, or of being opposed to real and lawful liberty. The Church, indeed, deems it unlawful to place the various forms of Divine Worship on the same footing as the true religion, but does not, on that account, condemn those rulers who for the sake of securing some great good, or of hindering some great evil, allow patiently custom or usage to be a kind of sanction for each kind of religion having its place in the State. And in

or the toleration of false religions;
fact the Church is wont to take earnest heed that no one shall be forced to embrace the Catholic faith against his will, for, as St. Augustine wisely reminds us, "Man cannot believe otherwise than of his own free will."

In the same way the Church cannot approve of that liberty which begets a contempt of the most sacred laws of God, and casts off the obedience due to lawful authority, for this is not liberty so much as license, and is most correctly styled by St. Augustine the "liberty of self-ruin," and by the Apostle St. Peter the *cloak of malice*.*

---
* 1 *Peter* ii. 16.

Indeed, since it is opposed to reason, it is a true slavery, *for whosoever committeth sin is the slave of sin.* * On the other hand that liberty is truly genuine, and to be sought after, which in regard to the individual does not allow men to be the slaves of error and of passion, the worst of all masters; which, too, in public administration guides the citizens in wisdom and provides for them increased means of well-being; and which, further, protects the State from foreign interference. <small>or a reasonable civil and political liberty;</small>

This honourable liberty, alone worthy of human beings, the Church approves most highly and has never slackened her endeavour to preserve, strong and unchanged, among nations. And in truth whatever in the State is of chief avail for the common welfare; whatever has been usefully established to curb the license of rulers who are opposed to the true interests of the people, or to keep in check the leading authorities from unwarrantably interfering in municipal or family affairs;—whatever tends to uphold the honour, manhood, and equal rights of individual citizens;—of all these things, as the monuments of past ages bear witness, the Catholic Church has always been the originator, the promoter, or the guardian. Ever therefore consistent with herself, while on the one hand she rejects that exorbitant liberty which in individuals and in nations ends in license or in thraldom, on the other hand, she willingly and most gladly welcomes whatever improvements the age brings forth, if these really secure the prosperity of life here below, which is as it were a stage in the journey to the life that will know no ending.

---

* 2 *John* viii. 34.

Therefore, when it is said that the Church is jealous of modern political systems, and that she repudiates the discoveries of modern research, the charge is a ridiculous and groundless calumny. Wild opinions she does repudiate, wicked and seditious projects she does condemn, together with that habit of mind which points to the beginning of a wilful departure from God. But as all truth must necessarily proceed from God, the Church recognises in all truth that is reached by research, a trace of the divine intelligence. And as all truth in the natural order is powerless to destroy belief in the teachings of revelation, but can do much to confirm it, and as every newly discovered truth may serve to further the knowledge or the praise of God, it follows that whatsoever spreads the range of knowledge will always be willingly and even joyfully welcomed by the Church. She will always encourage and promote, as she does in other branches of knowledge, all study occupied with the investigation of nature. In these pursuits, should the human intellect discover any thing not known before, the Church makes no opposition. She never objects to search being made for things that minister to the refinements and comforts of life. So far indeed from opposing these she is now, as she ever has been, hostile alone to indolence and sloth, and earnestly wishes that the talents of men may bear more and more abundant fruit by cultivation and exercise. Moreover she gives encouragement to every kind of art and handicraft, and through her influence, directing all strivings after progress towards virtue and salvation, she labours to prevent

or scientific research.

man's intellect and industry from turning him away from God and from heavenly things.

The aim of the Pontiff in renewing this assertion of Catholic truth.

All this, though so reasonable and full of counsel, finds little favour now-a-days when States not only refuse to conform to the rules of Christian wisdom, but seem even anxious to recede from them further and further on each successive day. Nevertheless, since truth when brought to light is wont, of its own nature, to spread itself far and wide, and gradually take possession of the minds of men, We, moved by the great and holy duty of Our Apostolic mission to all nations, speak, as We are bound to do, with freedom. Our eyes are not closed to the spirit of the times. We repudiate not the assured and useful improvements of our age, but devoutly wish affairs of State to take a safer course than they are now taking, and to rest on a more firm foundation without injury to the true freedom of the people. For the best parent and guardian of liberty amongst men is truth. *The truth shall make you free.* *

Duties of Catholics.

If in the difficult times in which our lot is cast, Catholics will give ear to Us, as it behoves them to do, they will readily see what are the duties of each one in matters of opinion as well as action. As regards opinion, whatever the Roman Pontiffs have hitherto taught, or shall hereafter teach, must be held with a firm grasp of mind, and, so often as occasion requires, must be openly professed.

---

* *John* viii. 32.

THE CHRISTIAN CONSTITUTION OF STATES. 95

with reference to opinions;

Especially with reference to the so-called "Liberties" which are so greatly coveted in these days, all must stand by the judgment of the Apostolic See, and have the same mind. Let no man be deceived by the outward appearance of these *liberties*, but let each one reflect whence these have had their origin, and by what efforts they are everywhere upheld and promoted. Experience has made us well acquainted with their results to the State, since everywhere they have borne fruits which the good and wise bitterly deplore. If there really exist anywhere, or if we in imagination conceive, a State, waging wanton and tyrannical war against Christianity, and if we compare with it the modern form of government just described, this latter may seem the more endurable of the two. Yet, undoubtedly, the principles on which such a government is grounded are, as we have said, of a nature which no one can approve.

in private life;

Secondly, action may relate to private and domestic matters, or to matters public. As to private affairs, the first duty is to conform life and conduct to the gospel precepts, and to refuse to shrink from this duty when Christian virtue demands some sacrifice difficult to make. All, moreover, are bound to love the Church as their common mother, to obey her laws, promote her honour, defend her rights, and to endeavour to make her respected and loved by those over whom they have authority. It is also of great moment

in their public capacity.

to the public welfare to take a prudent part in the business of municipal administration, and to endeavour above all to introduce effectual measures, so that, as becomes a Christian people, public provision may be made for the instruction of youth in religion and true morality. Upon these things the well-being of every State greatly depends.

Furthermore it is in general fitting and salutary that Catholics should extend their efforts beyond this restricted sphere, and give their attention to national politics. We say *in general*, because these Our precepts are addressed to all nations. However, it may in some places be true that, for most urgent and just reasons, it is by no means expedient for Catholics to engage in public affairs or to take an active part in politics. Nevertheless, as We have laid down, to take no share in public matters would be equally as wrong (We speak in general) as not to have concern for, or not to bestow labour upon, the common good. And this all the more because Catholics are admonished, by the very doctrines which they profess, to be upright and faithful in the discharge of duty, while if they hold aloof, men whose principles offer but small guarantee for the welfare of the State, will the more readily seize the reins of government. This would tend also to the injury of the Christian religion, forasmuch as those would come into power who are badly disposed towards the Church, and those who are willing to befriend her would be deprived of all influence.

It follows therefore clearly that Catholics have just reasons for taking part in the conduct of public affairs.

For in so doing they assume not the responsibility of approving what is blameworthy in the actual methods of government, but seek to turn these very methods, so far as is possible, to the genuine and true public good, and to use their best endeavours at the same time to infuse as it were into all the veins of the State the healthy sap and blood of Christian wisdom and virtue. The morals and ambitions of the heathens differed widely from those of the Gospel, yet Christians were to be seen living undefiled everywhere in the midst of pagan superstition, and, while always true to themselves, coming to the front boldly wherever an opening was presented. Models of loyalty to their rulers, submissive, so far as was permitted, to the sovereign power, they shed around them on every side a halo of sanctity; they strove to be helpful to their brethren, and to attract others to the wisdom of Jesus Christ, yet were bravely ready to withdraw from public life, nay, even to lay down their life, if they could not without loss of virtue retain honours, dignities, and offices. For this reason Christian ways and manners speedily found their way not only into private houses but into the camp, the Senate, and even into the imperial palaces. "We are but of yesterday," wrote Tertullian, "yet we swarm in all your institutions, we crowd your cities, islands, villages, towns, assemblies, the army itself, your wards and corporations, the palace, the senate, and the law courts." So that the Christian faith, when once it became lawful to make public profession of the gospel, appeared in most of the cities of Europe, not like an infant crying in its cradle, but already grown up and full of vigour.

Example of the early Christians.

In these our days it is well to revive these examples of our forefathers. First and foremost it is the duty of all Catholics worthy of the name and wishful to be

Recommendation to Catholics to remain well affected to the Church, and to be conformed to her mind; known as most loving children of the Church; to reject without swerving whatever is inconsistent with so fair a title; to make use of popular institutions, so far as can honestly be done, for the advancement of truth and righteousness; to strive that liberty of action shall not transgress the bounds marked out by nature and the law of God; to endeavour to bring back all Civil society to the pattern and form of Christianity which We have described. It is barely possible to lay down any fixed method by which such purposes are to be attained, because the means adopted must suit places and times widely differing from one another. Nevertheless, above all things, unity of aim must be preserved, and similarity must be sought after in all plans of action. Both these objects will be carried into effect without fail, if all will follow the guidance of the Apostolic See as their rule of life, and obey the bishops whom the Holy Ghost has placed to rule the Church of God.* The defence of Catholicism, indeed, necessarily demands that in the profession of doctrines taught by the Church all shall be of one mind and all steadfast in believing; and care must be taken never to connive, in any way, at false opinions, never to withstand them less strenuously than truth allows. In mere matters of opinion it is permissible to discuss things with moderation, with a

to be unanimous in the profession of the doctrines taught by the Church;

---

* *Acts* xx. 28.

desire of searching into the truth, without unjust suspicion or angry recriminations.

to reject whatever is akin to Naturalism or Rationalism,

Hence, lest concord be broken by rash charges, let this be understood by all, that the integrity of Catholic faith cannot be reconciled with opinions verging on Naturalism or Rationalism, the essence of which is utterly to sterilise Christianity, and to instal in society the supremacy of man to the exclusion of God. Further,

or divorces public from private duty ;

it is unlawful to follow one line of conduct in private and another in public, respecting privately the authority of the Church, but publicly rejecting it : for this would amount to joining together good and evil, and to putting man in conflict with himself; whereas he ought always to be consistent, and never in the least point nor in any condition of life to swerve from Christian virtue.

But in matters merely political, as for instance the best form of government, and this or that system of administration, a difference of opinion is lawful. Those, therefore, whose piety is in other respects known, and whose minds are ready to accept in all obedience the decrees of the Apostolic See, cannot in justice be accounted as bad men because they disagree as to subjects We have mentioned ; and still graver wrong will be done them, if—as We have more than once perceived with regret—they are accused of violating, or of wavering in, the Catholic faith.

Let this be well borne in mind by all who are in the habit of publishing their opinions, and above all by journalists. In the endeavour to secure interests of the highest order there is no room for intestine strife or party rivalries; since all should aim with one mind and purpose to make safe that which is the common object of all,—the maintenance of Religion and of the State.

foregoing all domestic controversies, especially in the periodical press.
If, therefore, there have hitherto been dissensions, let them henceforth be gladly buried in oblivion. If rash or injurious acts have been committed, whoever may have been at fault, let mutual charity make amends, and let the past be redeemed by a special submission of all to the Apostolic See.

In this way Catholics will attain two most excellent results: they will become helpers to the Church in preserving and propagating Christian wisdom; and they will confer the greatest benefit on Civil society, the safety of which is exceedingly imperilled by evil teachings and bad passions.

This, Venerable Brethren, is what We have thought it Our duty to expound to all nations of the Catholic world touching the Christian Constitution of States and the duties of individual citizens.

It behoves Us now with earnest prayer to implore the protection of Heaven, beseeching God, Who alone can enlighten the minds of men and move their will, to bring about those happy ends for which We yearn and strive, for His greater glory and the general salvation of mankind. As a happy augury of the divine benefits, and in token of Our paternal benevolence, to you, Venerable Brothers, and to the clergy and to the whole people committed to your charge and vigilance, We grant lovingly in the Lord the Apostolic Benediction.

ON THE CHIEF DUTIES OF CHRISTIANS AS CITIZENS.

Encyclical Letter, January 10, 1890.

FROM day to day it becomes more and more evident how needful it is that the principles of Christian Wisdom should be ever borne in mind, and that the life, the morals, and the institutions of nations should be wholly conformed to them. From the fact of these principles having been disregarded, mischiefs so vast have accrued, that no right-minded man can face the trials of the time being without grave solicitude, nor contemplate the future without serious alarm. Progress, not inconsiderable indeed, has been made towards securing the well-being of the body and of material things; but all natural advantages that administer to the senses of man, while bringing in their train the possession of wealth, power, and limitless resources, may indeed greatly avail to procure the comforts and increase the enjoyments of life, but are incapable of satisfying the soul created for higher and more glorious benefits. To fix the gaze on God, and to aim earnestly at becoming like Him, is the supreme law of the life of man. For we

<small>The evil of neglecting Christian teaching.</small>

<small>Material progress cannot lead man to his last end.</small>

were created in the Divine image and likeness, and are vehemently urged, by our very nature, to return to Him from Whom we have origin. But not by bodily motion or effort do we make advance towards God, but through acts of the soul, that is, through knowledge and love. God is, in very deed, the primal and supreme truth, and truth the food on which alone the soul is nourished; and God is holiness in perfection and the sovereign good, to which solely the will may aspire and which it may attain, when virtue is its guide.

But what applies to individual men applies equally to society—domestic alike and civil. Nature did not fashion society with intent that man should seek in it his last end, but that in it and through it he should find suitable aids whereby to attain to his own perfection. If then a civil government strives after external advantages merely, and the attainment of such objects as adorn life; if in administering public affairs it is wont to put God aside, and show no solicitude for the upholding of moral law; it deflects wofully from its right course and from the injunctions of nature: nor should such a gathering together and association of men be accounted as a commonwealth, but only as a deceitful imitation and make-believe of Civil organization.

A godless government deserves not the name.

As to what We have termed the well-being of the soul, which consists chiefly in the practice of the true religion and unswerving observance of the Christian precepts, We perceive that it is daily losing esteem among men, either by reason of forgetfulness or disregard, in such

The decline of religion owing to the pursuit of temporal advantages.

wise that the greater the advance made in the well-being of the body, the greater is the falling away in that of the soul. A striking proof of the lessening and enfeebling of Christian faith is seen in the insults that are, alas! so frequently, in open day, and before Our very eyes, offered to the Catholic Church—insults, indeed, to which an age cherishing religion would on no account have submitted. For these reasons how great a multitude of men is involved in danger as to their eternal salvation surpasses belief; but more than this, nations and even vast empires themselves cannot long remain unharmed, since, upon the lapsing of Christian institutions and morality, the main foundation of human society must necessarily be uprooted. Force alone will remain to preserve public tranquillity and order; force, however, is very feeble when the bulwark of religion has been removed; and being more apt to beget slavery than obedience, it bears within itself the germs of ever increasing troubles. The present century has encountered notable disasters, nor is it clear that some equally terrible are not impending. The very times in which we live are warning us to seek remedies there where alone they are to be found—namely, by re-establishing in the family circle and throughout the whole range of society the doctrines and practices of the Christian religion. In this lies the sole means of freeing us from the ills now weighing us down, of forestalling the dangers now threatening the world. For the

The object of this encyclical letter.

accomplishment of this end, Venerable Brothers, We must bring to bear all the activity and diligence that lie within Our power. Although We have already, under other circumstances, and whenever occasion required, treated of these matters in other Letters, We deem it expedient, in this message to you, to define more in detail the duties of Catholics, inasmuch as these would, if strictly observed, avail with wondrous power to save society in all its length and breadth. We are engaged, as regards matters of highest moment, in a violent and well-nigh daily struggle, wherein it is hard at times for the minds of many not to be deluded, not to go astray, not to yield. It behoves Us, Venerable Brothers, to warn, instruct and exhort each of the faithful with an earnestness befitting the occasion: *that none may abandon the way of truth.*

It cannot be doubted that duties more numerous and of greater moment devolve on Catholics than upon such as are either not sufficiently enlightened in relation to the Catholic faith, or who are entirely unacquainted with its doctrines. Considering that forthwith upon salvation being wrought out for mankind, Jesus Christ laid upon His Apostles the injunction to *preach the Gospel to every creature*, He imposed, it is evident, upon all men the duty of learning thoroughly and believing what they were taught. This duty is intimately bound up with the gaining of eternal salvation: *He that believeth and is baptized shall be saved; but he that believeth not, shall be condemned.* * But the man who has embraced the

<small>Catholics, as children of the Church, have imperative duties towards her.</small>

---

* *Mark* xvi. 16.

Christian faith, as in duty bound, is by that very fact a subject of the Church as one of the children born of her, and becomes a member of that greatest and holiest Body, which it is the special charge of the Roman Pontiff to rule with supreme power, under its invisible Head, Christ Jesus. Now, if the natural law enjoins us to love devotedly and to defend the country in which we had birth, and in which we were brought up, so that every good citizen hesitates not to face death for his native land, very much more is it the urgent duty of Christians to be ever quickened by like feelings towards the Church. For the Church is the holy City of the living God, born of God Himself, and by Him built up and established. Upon this earth indeed she accomplishes her pilgrimage, but by instructing and guiding men, she summons them to eternal happiness. We are bound then to love dearly the country whence we have received the means of enjoyment this mortal life affords, but we have a much more urgent obligation to love, with ardent love, the Church to which we owe the life of the soul, a life that will endure for ever. For fitting it is to prefer the good of the soul to the well-being of the body, inasmuch as duties toward God are of a far more hallowed character than those toward men.

The duty of loving the Church and the State.

The love of Church and country, coming from God, cannot be opposed to each other.

Moreover, if we would judge aright, the supernatural love for the Church and the natural love of our own country proceed from the same eternal principle, since God Himself is their Author and originating Cause. Consequently it follows that between the duties they respectively enjoin, neither can come into collision with the other. We can, certainly, and should love ourselves, bear ourselves kindly towards our fellow-men, nourish affection for the State and the governing powers; but at the same time we can and must cherish toward the Church a feeling of filial piety, and love God with the deepest love of which we are capable. The order of precedence of these duties is, however, at times, either under stress of public calamities, or through the perverse will of men, inverted. For instances occur where the State seems to require from men as subjects one thing, and Religion, from men as Christians, quite another; and this in reality without any other ground, than that the rulers of the State either hold the sacred power of the Church of no account, or endeavour to subject it to their own will. Hence arises a conflict, and an occasion, through such conflict, of virtue being put to the proof. The two powers are confronted and urge their behests in a contrary sense; to obey both is wholly impossible. *No man can serve two masters,** for to please the one amounts to contemning the other. As to which should be preferred no one ought to balance for an instant. It is a high crime indeed to withdraw allegiance from God in order to please men; an act of consummate wickedness to break the laws of Jesus Christ, in order to yield obedience to earthly rulers, or, under pretext of keeping the Civil law, to ignore the rights of the

<small>The State has no right to order things opposed to God's law.</small>

---

* *Matthew* vi. 24.

Church; *we ought to obey God rather than men.* [*]
This answer, which of old Peter and the other Apostles were used to give the Civil authorities who enjoined unrighteous things, we must, in like circumstances, give always and without hesitation. No better citizen is there, whether in time of peace or war, than the Christian who is mindful of his duty; but such a one should be ready to suffer all things, even death itself, rather than abandon the cause of God or of the Church.

Hence they who blame, and call by the name of sedition, this steadfastness of attitude in the choice of duty, have not rightly apprehended the force and nature of true law. We are speaking of matters widely known, and which We have before now more than once fully explained. Law is of its very essence a mandate of right reason, proclaimed by a properly constituted authority, for the common good. But true and legitimate authority is void of sanction, unless it proceed from God the supreme Ruler and Lord of all. The Almighty alone can commit power to a man over his fellow-men; nor may that be accounted as right reason which is in disaccord with truth and with divine reason; nor that held to be true good which is repugnant to the supreme and unchangeable good, or that wrests aside and draws away the wills of men from the charity of God.

Catholics strictly bound to obey the government in things not contrary to divine authority. Hallowed therefore in the mind of Christians is the very idea of public authority, in which they recognise some likeness and symbol as it were of the Divine Majesty, even when it is exercised

---

* *Acts* v. 29.

by one unworthy. A just and due reverence to the laws abides in them, not from force and threats, but from a consciousness of duty; *for God hath not given us the spirit of fear.* *

But if the laws of the State are manifestly at variance with the Divine Law, containing enactments hurtful to the Church, or conveying injunctions adverse to the duties imposed by religion, or if they violate in the person of the supreme Pontiff the authority of Jesus Christ, then truly, to resist becomes a positive duty, to obey, a crime; a crime moreover combined with misdemeanour against the State itself, inasmuch as every offence levelled against religion is also a sin against the State. Here anew it becomes evident how unjust is the reproach of sedition: for the obedience due to rulers and legislators is not refused; but there is a deviation from their will in those precepts only which they have no power to enjoin. Commands that are issued adversely to the honour due to God, and hence are beyond the scope of justice, must be looked upon as anything rather than laws. You are fully aware, Venerable Brothers, that this is the very contention of the Apostle St. Paul, who, in writing to Titus, after reminding Christians that they are *to be subject to princes and powers, and to obey at a word*, at once adds, *And to be ready to every good work.* † Thereby he openly declares that if laws of men contain injunctions contrary to the eternal law of God, it is right not to obey them. In like manner

<small>Laws invalid which are against those of God.</small>

---

* 2 *Timothy* i. 7. † *Tit.* iii. 1.

the Prince of the Apostles, gave this courageous and sublime answer to those who would have deprived him of the liberty of preaching the Gospel: *If it be just in the sight of God to hear you rather than God, judge ye, for we cannot but speak the things which we have seen and heard.**

Wherefore, to love both countries, that of earth below and that of Heaven above, yet in such mode that the love of our heavenly surpass the love of our earthly home, and that human laws be never set above the Divine Law, is the essential duty of Christians, and the fountain-head, so to say, from which all other duties spring. The Redeemer of mankind of Himself has said : *For this was I born, and for this came I into the world, that I should give testimony to the truth.*† In like manner, *I am come to cast fire upon earth, and what will I but that it be kindled?*‡ In the knowledge of this truth, which constitutes the highest perfection of the mind ; in divine charity which, in like manner, completes the will, all Christian life and liberty abide. This noble patrimony of truth and charity entrusted by Jesus Christ to the Church, she defends and maintains ever with untiring endeavour and watchfulness.

But with what bitterness and in how many guises war has been waged against the Church, it would be ill-timed now to urge. From the fact that it has been vouchsafed to human reason to snatch from nature, **Scientific progress used against the Church.** through the investigations of science, many of her treasured secrets and to apply them befittingly to the divers requirements of

---
* *Acts* iv. 19, 20. † *John* xviii. 37. ‡ *Luke* xii. 49.

life, men have become possessed with so arrogant a sense of their own powers, as already to consider themselves able to banish from social life the authority and empire of God. Led away by this delusion, they make over to human nature the dominion of which they think God has been despoiled; from nature, they maintain, we must seek the principle and rule of all truth; from nature they aver, alone spring, and to it should be referred, all the duties that religious feeling prompts. Hence they deny all revelation from on High, and all fealty due to the Christian teaching of morals as well as all obedience to the Church; and they go so far as to deny her power of making laws and exercising every other kind of right, even disallowing the Church any place among the civil institutions of the State. These men aspire unjustly, and with their might strive, to gain control over public affairs and lay hands on the rudder of the State, in order that the legislation may the more easily be adapted to these principles, and the morals of the people influenced in accordance with them. Whence it comes to pass that in many countries Catholicism is either openly assailed or else secretly interfered with, full impunity being granted to the most pernicious doctrines, while the public profession of Christian truth is shackled often-times with manifold constraints.

Enmity to Christ and the Church is born of pride.

Under such evil circumstances therefore each one is bound in conscience to watch over himself, taking all means possible to preserve the faith inviolate in the depths of his soul, avoiding all risks, and arming himself on all occasions, especially against the various

Need of Catholics to be well instructed in their religion. specious sophisms rife among non-believers. In order to safeguard this virtue of faith in its integrity, We declare it to be very profitable and consistent with the requirements of the time, that each one, according to the measure of his capacity and intelligence, should make a deep study of Christian doctrine, and imbue his mind with as perfect a knowledge as may be of those matters that are interwoven with religion and lie within the range of reason. And as it is necessary that faith should not only abide untarnished in the soul, but should grow with ever painstaking increase, the suppliant and humble entreaty of the Apostles ought constantly to be addressed to God: *Increase our faith.* *

Catholics should be ready, and anxious, to defend the faith. But in this same matter, touching Christian faith, there are other duties, whose exact and religious observance, necessary at all times in the interests of eternal salvation, become more especially so in these our days. Amid such reckless and wide-spread folly of opinion it is, as We have said, the office of the Church to undertake the defence of truth and uproot errors from the mind, and this charge has to be at all times sacredly observed by her, seeing that the honour of God and the salvation of men are confided to her keeping. But when necessity compels, not those only who are invested with power of rule are bound to safeguard the integrity of faith, but, as St. Thomas maintains, "Each one is under obligation to show forth his faith, either to instruct and encourage others of the faithful,

---

* *Luke* xviii. 5.

or to repel the attacks of unbelievers."* To recoil before an enemy, or to keep silence, when from all sides such clamours are raised against truth, is the part of a man either devoid of character, or who entertains doubt as to the truth of what he professes to believe. In both cases such mode of behaving is base and is insulting to God, and both are incompatible with the salvation of mankind. This kind of conduct is profitable only to the enemies of the faith, for nothing emboldens the wicked so greatly as the lack of courage on the part of the good. Moreover, want of vigour on the part of Christians is so much the more blameworthy, as not seldom little would be needed on their part to bring to naught false charges and refute erroneous opinions; and always by exerting themselves more strenuously they might reckon upon being successful. After all, no one can be prevented from putting forth that strength of soul which is the characteristic of true Christians; and very frequently by such display of courage our enemies lose heart and their designs are thwarted. Christians are, moreover, born for combat, whereof the greater the vehemence, the more assured, God aiding, the triumph: *Have confidence; I have overcome the world.*† Nor is there any ground for alleging that Jesus Christ, the Guardian and Champion of the Church, needs not in any manner the help of men. Power certainly is not wanting to Him, but in His loving-kindness He would assign to us a share in

<small>To defend the Church is the duty and glory of all Catholics.</small>

---

* 2a 2æ Q. iii. a. 2 ad 2.   † *John* xvi. 33.

obtaining and applying the fruits of salvation procured through His grace.

Catholics should profess and spread the Faith.

The chief elements of this duty consist in professing openly and unflinchingly the Catholic doctrine, and in propagating it to the utmost of our power. For, as is often said, and with most great truth, there is nothing so hurtful to Christian wisdom as that it should not be known, since it possesses, when loyally received, inherent power to drive away error. So soon as Catholic truth is apprehended by a simple and unprejudiced soul, reason yields assent. Now faith, as a virtue, is a great boon of divine grace and goodness; nevertheless, the objects themselves to which faith is to be applied are scarcely known in any other way than through the hearing. *How shall they believe Him of whom they have not heard? and how shall they hear without a preacher? Faith then cometh by hearing, and hearing by the word of Christ.* * Since then faith is necessary for salvation, it follows that the word of Christ must be preached. The

Faith cometh by hearing, hence the preaching of the Word by the Pastors of the Church.

office indeed of preaching, that is of teaching, lies by divine right in the province of the pastors, namely of the bishops whom *the Holy Ghost has placed to rule the Church of God.* † It belongs above all to the Roman Pontiff, Vicar of Jesus Christ, established as head of the universal Church, teacher of all that pertains to morals and faith. No one, however, must entertain the notion that private individuals are

---

* *Rom.* x. 14, 17. † *Acts* xx. 28.

<small>Private individuals ought to help in this teaching.</small> prevented from taking some active part in this duty of teaching, especially those on whom God has bestowed gifts of mind with the strong wish of rendering themselves useful. These, so often as circumstances demand, may take upon themselves, not indeed the office of the pastor, but the task of communicating to others what they have themselves received, becoming, as it were, living echoes of their masters in the faith. Such co-operation on the part of the laity has seemed to the Fathers of the Vatican Council so opportune and fruitful of good that they thought well to invite it. "All faithful Christians, but those chiefly who are in a prominent position, or engaged in teaching, we entreat, by the compassion

<small>Witness of the Council Vatican on this point.</small> of Jesus Christ, and enjoin by the authority of the same God and Saviour, that they bring aid to ward off and eliminate these errors from Holy Church, and contribute their zealous help in spreading abroad the light of undefiled faith.* Let each one therefore bear in mind that he both can and should, so far as may be, preach the Catholic faith by the authority of his example, and by open and constant profession of the

<small>Every one bound to preach by example and profession of the Faith.</small> obligations it imposes. In respect consequently to the duties that bind us to God and the Church, it should be borne earnestly in mind that in propagating Christian truth and warding off errors, the zeal of the laity should, as far as possible, be brought actively into play.

---

* Const. *Dei Filius*, sub fine.

The faithful would not, however, so completely and advantageously satisfy these duties as is fitting they should, were they to enter the field as isolated champions of the faith. Jesus Christ indeed has clearly intimated that the hostility and hatred of men, which He first and foremost experienced, would be shown in like degree towards the work founded by Him, so that many would be barred from profiting by the salvation for which all are indebted to His loving-kindness. Wherefore He willed not only to train disciples in His doctrine,

<small>Common action a duty, from the very constitution of the Church.</small>

but to unite them into one Society, and fastly conjoin them in one Body, *which is the Church,* * whereof He would be the Head. The life of Jesus Christ pervades therefore the entire framework of this body, cherishes and nourishes its every member, uniting each with each, and making all work together to the same end, albeit the action of each be not the same. † Hence it follows that not only is the Church a perfect society far excelling every other, but it is enjoined by her Founder that for the salvation of mankind she is to contend *as an army drawn up in battle array.* ‡ The organization and constitution of Christian society can in no wise be changed, neither can any one of its members live as he may choose, nor elect that mode of fighting which best pleases him. For in effect he scatters and gathers not, who gathers not with the Church and with Jesus Christ;

---

* *Coloss.* i. 24.

† *As in one body we have many members, but all the members have not the same office.—Rom.* xii. 4, 5.

‡ *Canticles* vi. 9.

and all who fight not jointly with Him and with the Church, are in very truth contending against God.*

Concord of opinion a prime need. To bring about such an union of minds and uniformity of action— not without reason so greatly feared by the enemies of Catholicism,—the main point is that a perfect harmony of opinion should prevail; in which intent we find Paul the Apostle exhorting the Corinthians with earnest zeal and solemn weight of words: *Now I beseech you, brethren, by the name of our Lord Jesus Christ, that you all speak the same thing, and that there be no schisms among you: but that you be perfectly in the same mind, and in the same judgment.* †

The wisdom of this precept is readily apprehended. In truth, thought is the principle of action, and hence there cannot exist agreement of will, nor similarity of action, if people all think differently one from the other.

In the case of those who profess to take reason as their sole guide, there would hardly be found, if, indeed, there ever could be found, unity of doctrine. Indeed, the art of knowing things as they really are is exceedingly difficult; moreover, the mind of man is by nature feeble and drawn this way and that by a variety of opinions, and not seldom led astray by impressions coming from without; and furthermore, the influence of the passions oftentimes takes away, or certainly at least diminishes, the capacity for grasping

Independence of mind the source of discord even in the natural order.

---

* *Who is not with Me, is against Me, and he who gathereth not with Me, scattereth.—Luke* xi. 22.

† 1 *Corinthians* i. 10.

the truth. On this account, in controlling State affairs means are often taken to keep those together by force, who cannot agree in their way of thinking.

Perfect religious concord is of divine precept. It happens far otherwise with Christians: they receive their rule of faith from the Church, by whose authority and under whose guidance they are conscious that they have beyond question attained to truth. Consequently as the Church is one, because Jesus Christ is one, so throughout the whole Christian world there is, and ought to be, but one doctrine: *One Lord, one faith;* * *but having the same spirit of faith*,† they possess the saving principle whence proceed spontaneously one and the same will in all, and one and the same tenour of action.

Now, as the Apostle Paul urges, this unanimity ought to be perfect. Christian faith reposes not on human but on divine authority, for what God has revealed "we believe not on account of the intrinsic evidence of the truth perceived by the natural light of our reason, but on account of the authority of God revealing, Who cannot be deceived nor Himself deceive." ‡ It follows as a consequence, that whatever things are manifestly revealed by God, we must receive with a similar and equal assent. To refuse to believe any one of them is equivalent to rejecting them all; for those at once destroy the very groundwork of faith, who deny that God has spoken to men, or who bring into doubt His infinite truth and wisdom. To determine however which

---

* *Ephes.* iv. 5.   † 2 *Cor.* iv. 13.   ‡ Conc. Vat. Const. *Dei Filius.*

are the doctrines divinely revealed, belongs to the teaching Church, to whom God has entrusted the safe-keeping and interpretation of His utterances. But the supreme Teacher in the Church is the Roman Pontiff. Union of minds, therefore requires, together with a perfect accord in the one faith, complete submission and obedience of will to the Church and to the Roman Pontiff, as to God Himself. This obedience should, however, be perfect, because it is enjoined by faith itself, and has this in common with faith, that it cannot be given in shreds;—nay, were it not absolute and perfect in every particular, it might wear the name of obedience, but its essence would disappear. Christian usage attaches such value to this perfection of obedience, that it has been, and will ever be, accounted the distinguishing mark by which we are able to recognise Catholics. Admirably does the following passage from St. Thomas of Aquin set before us the right view: "The formal object of faith is primary truth, as it is shown forth in the Holy Scriptures, and in the teaching of the Church, which proceeds from the fountain-head of truth. It follows, therefore, that he who does not adhere, as to an infallible divine rule, to the teaching of the Church which proceeds from the primary truth manifested in the Holy Scriptures, possesses not the habit of faith: but matters of faith he holds otherwise than through faith. Now it is evident that he who clings

By obedience to the teaching Church revelation is made known to us.

Obedience if not complete does not exist.

St. Thomas of Aquin on this matter.

to the doctrines of the Church as to an infallible rule, yields his assent to everything the Church teaches; but otherwise, if with reference to what the Church teaches, he holds what he likes, but does not hold what he does not like, he adheres not to the teaching of the Church, as to an infallible rule, but to his own will." *

"The faith of the whole Church should be one, according to the precept (1 *Corinthians* i.): *Let all speak the same thing, and let there be no schisms among you;* and this cannot be observed save on condition that questions which arise touching faith should be determined by him who presides over the whole Church, whose sentence must consequently be accepted without wavering. And hence to the sole authority of the Supreme Pontiff does it pertain to publish a new revision of the Symbol, as also to decree all other matters that concern the Universal Church." †

In defining the limits of the obedience owed to the Pastors of souls, but most of all to the authority of the Roman Pontiff, it must not be supposed that it is only to be yielded in relation to dogmas of which the obstinate denial cannot be disjoined from the crime of heresy. Nay, further, it is not enough sincerely and firmly to assent to doctrines which, though not defined by any solemn pronouncement of the Church, are by her proposed to belief, as divinely revealed, in her common and universal teaching, and which the Vatican Council declared are to be believed *with Catholic and Divine Faith.* But this likewise must be reckoned amongst the duties of Christians, that they allow them-

---

* 2a 2æ, q. v. art. 3.   † Ibid. q. i. art. 10.

selves to be ruled and directed by the authority and leadership of Bishops, and above all of the Apostolic See. And how fitting it is that this should be so, any one can easily perceive. For the things contained in the Divine Oracles have reference to God in part, and in part to man, and to whatever is necessary for the attainment of his eternal salvation. Now, both these, that is to say, what we are bound to believe, and what we are obliged to do, are laid down, as we have stated, by the Church using her divine right, and in the Church by the Supreme Pontiff. Wherefore, it belongs to the Pope to judge authoritatively what things the Sacred Oracles contain, as well as what doctrines are in harmony, and what in disagreement, with them; and also, for the same reason, to show forth what things are to be accepted as right, and what to be rejected as worthless; what it is necessary to do and what to avoid doing, in order to attain to eternal salvation. For, otherwise, there would be no sure interpreter of the commands of God, nor would there be any safe guide showing man the way he should live.*

---

* The following note will perhaps help to make clearer the words of His Holiness, which, clear enough in themselves, may be found somewhat obscure by those unaccustomed to use theological terms. It is evident that articles defined to be of faith can be accepted wholly, and at all points, by those alone who believe all doctrines flowing immediately from what is of faith, or closely connected with it. For these doctrines are propounded to belief by the Church in her ordinary and universal teaching. Though not defined as of faith, they are to be held with "Catholic and Divine Faith." To deny them would lead to danger of making shipwreck of the faith, since they are not only certain, but are declared by the Church to be certain. We are

In addition to what has been laid down, it is necessary to enter more fully into the nature of the Church. She is not an association of Christians brought together by chance, but is a divinely established and admirably constituted Society, having for its direct and proximate purpose to lead the world to peace and holiness. And since the Church alone has, through the Grace of God, received the means necessary to realize such end, she has her fixed laws, special spheres of action, and a certain method, fixed and conformable to her nature, of governing Christian peoples. But the exercise of such governing power is difficult, and leaves room for numberless conflicts, inasmuch as the Church rules peoples scattered through every portion of the earth, differing in race and customs, who, living under the sway of the laws of their respective country, owe obedience alike to the civil and religious authorities. The duties enjoined are incumbent on the same persons, as already stated, and between them there exists neither contradiction nor confusion; for

What is included in this complete obedience to the Church.

There is no antagonism between Church and State.

---

therefore bound to accept them, and to submit ourselves to such decisions concerning doctrine as are given by the Roman Pontiff or by Roman Congregations appointed by him. It is a sign of a mind being out of touch with the Church, to reject doctrines generally taught by theologians and Catholic doctors. The Vatican Council has declared that it is not enough to shun the self-willed obstinacy of heresy, but we must carefully turn a deaf ear to those errors which, more or less nearly, approach heresy; and all Christians are warned that they are in duty bound to observe the Constitutions and Decrees by which the Holy See has proscribed perverse opinions of whatever kind. [*Editor.*]

some of these duties have relation to the prosperity of the State, others refer to the general good of the Church, and both have as their object to train men to perfection.

The tracing out of these rights and duties being thus set forth, it is plainly evident that the governing powers are wholly free to carry out the business of the State; and this, not only not against the wish of the Church, but manifestly with her co-operation, inasmuch as she strongly urges to the practice of piety, which implies right feeling towards God, and by that very fact inspires a right-mindedness towards the rulers in the State. The spiritual power, however, has a far loftier purpose, the Church directing her aim to govern the minds of men in the defending of the *Kingdom of God, and His justice*, * a task she is wholly bent upon accomplishing.

<small>The Church, exacting obedience from Rulers, helps them to govern.</small>

No one can, however, without risk to faith, foster any doubt as to the Church alone having been invested with such power of governing souls as to exclude altogether the civil authority. In truth it was not to Cæsar but to Peter that Jesus Christ entrusted the Keys of the Kingdom of Heaven. From this doctrine touching the relations of politics and religion, originate important consequences which We cannot pass over in silence.

A notable difference exists between every kind of Civil rule and that of the Kingdom of Christ. If this latter bear a certain likeness and character to a Civil kingdom,

---

* *Matt.* vi. 33.

it is distinguished from it by its origin, principle, and essence. The Church, therefore, possesses the right to exist and to protect herself by institutions and laws in accordance with her nature. And since she not only is a perfect Society in herself, but superior to every other society of human growth, she resolutely refuses, prompted alike by right and by duty, to link herself to any mere party and to subject herself to the fleeting exigencies of politics. On like grounds the Church, the guardian always of her own right and most observant of that of others, holds that it is not her province to decide which is the best amongst many diverse forms of Government and the Civil institutions of Christian States, and amid the various kinds of State rule she does not disapprove of any, provided the respect due to religion and the observance of good morals be upheld. By such standard of conduct should the thoughts and mode of acting of every Catholic be directed. There is no doubt but that in the sphere of politics ample matter may exist for legitimate difference of opinion, and that, the single reserve being made of the rights of justice and truth, all may strive to bring into actual working the ideas believed likely to be more conducive than others to the general welfare. But to attempt to involve the Church in party strife, and seek to bring her support to bear against those who take opposite views, is only worthy of partisans. Religion should, on the contrary, be accounted by every one as holy and inviolate;—nay, in the public order itself of States—which cannot be

The Church approves of all lawful forms of Civil government.

severed from the laws influencing morals and from religious duties—it is always urgent, and indeed the main pre-occupation, to take thought how best to consult the interests of Catholicism. Wherever these appear by reason of the efforts of adversaries to be in danger, all differences of opinion among Catholics should forthwith cease, so that, like thoughts and counsels prevailing, they may hasten to the aid of religion, the general and supreme good, to which all else should be referred. We think it well to treat this matter somewhat more in detail.

All should imitate the Church in this respect.

The Church alike and the State, doubtless, both possess individual sovereignty; hence, in the carrying out of public affairs, neither obeys the other within the limits to which each is restricted by its Constitution. It does not hence follow, however, that Church and State are in any manner severed, and still less antagonistic. Nature, in fact, has given us not only physical existence, but moral life likewise. Hence, from the tranquillity of public order, whose immediate purpose is Civil society, man expects that this may be able to secure all his needful well-being, and still more supply the sheltering care which perfects his moral life, which consists mainly in the knowledge and practice of virtue. He wishes moreover at the same time, as in duty bound, to find in the Church the aids necessary to his religious perfection, which consists in the knowledge and practice of the true religion; of that religion which is the queen of virtues, because in binding these to God it completes them all and perfects them. Therefore they who are engaged in framing constitutions and in enacting laws should bear in mind the moral and religious nature of man, and take care to help him, but in a right and orderly way, to gain perfection, neither enjoining nor forbidding anything save what is reasonably consistent with Civil as well as with religious requirements. On this very account the Church cannot stand by, indifferent as to the import and significance of laws enacted by the State; not in so far indeed as they refer to the State, but in so far as, passing beyond their due limits, they trench upon the rights of the Church. From God has the duty been assigned to the Church, not only to interpose resistance, if at any time the State rule should run counter to religion, but further to make a strong endeavour that the power of the Gospel may pervade the law and institutions of the nations. And inasmuch as the destiny of the State depends mainly on the disposition of those who are at the head of affairs, it follows that the Church cannot give countenance or favour to those whom she knows to be imbued with a spirit of hostility to her; who refuse openly to respect her rights; who make it their aim and purpose to tear asunder the alliance that should, by the very nature of things, connect the interests of religion with those of the State. On the contrary she is (as she is bound to be) the upholder of those who are themselves imbued with the right way of thinking as to the relations between Church and State, and who strive to make them work in perfect accord for the common good. These precepts contain the abiding principle by which every Catholic

Civil law must keep in view the moral order.

Catholics should uphold Civil Rulers who favour Religion. should shape his conduct in regard to public life. In short, where the Church does not forbid taking part in public affairs, it is fit and proper to give support to men of acknowledged worth, and who pledge themselves to deserve well in the Catholic cause, and on no account may it be allowed to prefer to them any such individuals as are hostile to religion.

The enemies of the Church use against her dissensions amongst Catholics. Whence it appears how urgent is the duty to maintain perfect union of minds, especially at these our times, when the Christian name is assailed with designs so concerted and subtle. All who have it at heart to attach themselves earnestly to the Church, which is *the pillar and ground of the truth*,* will easily steer clear of masters who are *lying and promising them liberty, when they themselves are slaves of corruption*.† Nay, more, having made themselves sharers in the divine virtue which resides in the Church, they will triumph over the craft of their adversaries by wisdom, and over their violence by courage. This is not now the time and place to inquire whether and how far the inertness and internal dissensions of Catholics have contributed to the present condition of things; but it is certain at least that the perverse-minded would exhibit less boldness, and would not have brought about such an accumulation of ills, if the faith *which worketh by charity* ‡ had been generally more energetic and lively in the souls of men, and had there not been so universal

---

* 1 *Tim.* iii. 15.   † 2 *Peter* ii. 1, 19.   ‡ *Galat.* v. 6.

a drifting away from the divinely established rule of morality throughout Christianity. May at least the lessons afforded by the memory of the past have the good result of leading to a wiser mode of acting in the future.

Catholic statesmen should shun worldly prudence and rashness.

As to those who mean to take part in public affairs, they should avoid with the very utmost care two criminal excesses: so-called prudence and false courage. Some there are, indeed, who maintain that it is not opportune boldly to attack evil-doing in its might and when in the ascendant, lest, as they say, opposition should exasperate minds already hostile. These make it a matter of guess-work as to whether they are for the Church or against her; since on the one hand they give themselves out as professing the Catholic faith, and yet wish that the Church should allow certain opinions, at variance with her teaching, to be spread abroad with impunity.

The prudence of the flesh described.

They moan over the loss of faith and the perversion of morals, yet trouble themselves not to bring any remedy;—nay, not seldom, even add to the intensity of the mischief through too much forbearance or harmful dissembling. These same individuals would not have any one entertain a doubt as to their good will towards the Holy See; yet they have always a something by way of reproach against the Supreme Pontiff. The prudence of men of this cast is of that kind which is termed by the Apostle Paul *Wisdom of the flesh* and *death* of the soul, *because it is not subject to the law of God, neither can* *it be.* * Nothing is less calculated to amend such ills than prudence of this kind. For the enemies of the Church have for their object—and they hesitate not to proclaim it, and many among them boast of it—to destroy outright, if possible, the Catholic religion, which is alone the true religion. With such a purpose in hand they shrink from nothing; for they are fully conscious that the more faint-hearted those who withstand them become, the more easy will it be to work out their wicked will. Therefore they who cherish the *prudence of the flesh* and who pretend to be unaware that every Christian ought to be a valiant soldier of Christ; they who would fain obtain the rewards owing to conquerors, while they are leading the lives of cowards, untouched in the fight; are so far from thwarting the onward march of the evil-disposed, that on the contrary they even help it forward.

<small>How harmful it is to the cause of Christianity.</small>

On the other hand not a few, impelled by a false zeal, or—what is more blameworthy still—affecting sentiments which their conduct belies, take upon themselves to act a part which does not belong to them. They would fain see the Church's mode of action influenced by their ideas and their judgment, to such an extent that everything done otherwise they take ill or accept with repugnance. Some, yet again, expend their energies in fruitless contention, being worthy of blame equally with the former. To act in such manner is not to follow lawful authority but to forestal it, and unauthorised assume the duties

---

* *The wisdom of the flesh is an enemy to God; for it is not subject to the law of God, neither can it be.*—*Rom.* viii. 6, 7.

of the spiritual rulers, to the great detriment of the order which God established in His Church to be observed for ever, and which He does not permit to be violated with impunity by any one, whoever he may be.

The prudence of the spirit.

Honour then to those who shrink not from entering the arena, as often as need calls: believing and being convinced that the violence of injustice will be brought to an end and finally give way to the sanctity of right and religion! They truly seem invested with the dignity of time-honoured virtue, since they are struggling to defend religion, and chiefly against the faction banded together to attack Christianity with extreme daring and without tiring, and to pursue with incessant hostility the Sovereign Pontiff, fallen into their power. But men of this high character maintain without wavering the love of obedience, nor are they wont to undertake anything upon their own authority. Now, since a like resolve to obey, combined with constancy and sturdy courage, is needful, so that whatever trials the pressure of events may bring about, they may be *deficient in nothing*,* We greatly desire to fix deep in the minds of each one that which Paul calls the *wisdom of the spirit*,† for in controlling human actions this wisdom follows the excellent rule of moderation, with the happy result that no one either timidly despairs through lack of courage or presumes over-much from want of prudence. There is, however, a difference between the

State prudence consults the common good.

political prudence that relates to the general good, and that which concerns the good of individuals. This

---

* *James* i. 4. † *Rom.* viii. 6.

latter is shown forth in the case of private persons who obey the prompting of right reason in the direction of their own conduct; while the former is the characteristic of those who are set over others, and chiefly of rulers of the State, whose duty it is to exercise the power of command, so that the political prudence of private individuals would seem to consist wholly in carrying out faithfully the orders issued by lawful authority. *

It concerns above all others the Roman Pontiff; The like disposition and the same order should prevail in every Christian State by so much the more that the political prudence of the Pontiff embraces diverse and multiform things; for it is his charge not only to rule the Church, but generally so to regulate the actions of Christian Citizens that these may be in apt conformity to their hope of gaining eternal salvation. Whence it is clear that in addition to the complete accordance of thought and deed, the faithful

---

* "Prudence proceeds from reason, and to reason it specially pertains to guide and govern. Whence it follows that insomuch as any one takes part in the control and government of affairs, in so far ought he to be gifted with reason and prudence. But it is evident that the subject, so far as subject, and the servant, so far as servant, ought neither to control nor govern, but rather to be controlled and governed. Prudence then is not the special virtue of the servant, so far as servant, nor of the subject, so far as subject. But because any man, on account of his character of a reasonable being, may have some share in the government according to the degree which reason determines, it is fitting that in such proportion he should possess the virtue of prudence. Whence it manifestly results that prudence exists in the ruler, as it exists in the architect with regard to the building he has to construct, just as is expressed in the sixth Book of Morals, and that it exists in the subject, as it exists in the workman employed in the construction."—St. Thomas, 2a 2æ, Q. ii. 2, 4, 7, art. 12.

should imitate the practical political wisdom of the ecclesiastical authority. Now the administration of Christian affairs immediately under the Roman Pontiff appertains to the Bishops, who, although they attain not to the summit of pontifical power, are nevertheless truly princes in the ecclesiastical hierarchy; and as each one of them administers a particular church, they are " as master-workers . . . in the spiritual edifice,"* and they have members of the clergy to share their duties and carry out their decisions. Every one has to regulate his mode of conduct according to this constitution of the Church, which it is not in the power of any man to change. Consequently, just as in the exercise of their episcopal authority the bishops ought to be united with the Apostolic See, so should the members of the clergy and the laity live in close union with their Bishops. Among the Prelates indeed one or other there may be affording scope to criticism either in regard to personal conduct or in reference to opinions by him entertained about points of doctrine; but no private person may arrogate to himself the office of judge which Christ our Lord has bestowed on that one alone whom He placed in charge of His lambs and of His sheep. Let every one bear in mind that most wise teaching of Gregory the Great: "Subjects should be admonished not rashly to judge their prelates, even if they chance to see them acting in a blameworthy manner, lest reproving what is wrong, they be led by pride into greater wrong. They are to be warned against the danger of

then the Bishops.

It belongs to the Pope to judge the rulers of the Church.

---
* St. Thomas, Quodlib. I, xiv.

setting themselves up in audacious opposition to the superiors whose shortcomings they may notice. Should, therefore, the superiors really have committed grievous sins, their inferiors, penetrated with the fear of God, ought not to refuse them respectful submission. The actions of superiors should not be smitten by the sword of the word, even when they are rightly judged to have deserved censure." *

However, all endeavours will avail but little, unless our life be regulated conformably with the discipline of the Christian virtues. Let us call to mind what Holy Scripture records concerning the Jewish nation: *As long as they sinned not in the sight of their God, it was well with them, for their God hateth iniquity. And even . . . when they had revolted from the way that God had given them to walk therein, they were destroyed in battles by many nations.* † Now the nation of the Jews bore an inchoate semblance to the Christian people, and the vicissitudes of their history in olden times have often foreshadowed the truth that was to come; saving that God in His goodness has enriched and loaded us with far greater benefits, and on this account the sins of Christians are much greater, and bear the stamp of more shameful and criminal ingratitude.

The chief remedy is to be found in the practice of Christian virtue.

The Church, it is certain, at no time and in no particular is deserted by God; hence there is no reason why she should be alarmed at the wickedness of men; but in the case of nations falling away from Christian virtue there is not a like ground of assurance, *for sin maketh nations*

---

* *Reg. Pastor.* p. iii. cap. iv.   † *Judith* v. 21, 22.

miserable. * If every bygone age has experienced the force of this truth, wherefore should not our own? There are in truth very many signs which proclaim that just punishments are already menacing, and the condition of modern States tends to confirm this belief, since we perceive many of them in sad plight from intestine disorders, and not one entirely exempt. But should those leagued together in wickedness hurry onward in the road they have boldly chosen; should they increase in influence and power, in proportion as they make headway in their evil purposes and crafty schemes; there will be ground to fear lest the very foundations nature has laid for States to rest upon be utterly destroyed. Nor can such misgivings be removed by any mere human effort, especially as a vast number of men, having rejected the Christian faith, are on that account justly incurring the penalty of their pride, since blinded by their passions they search in vain for truth, laying hold on the false for the true, and thinking themselves wise when they call *evil good, and good evil,* and put *darkness in the place of light, and light in the place of darkness.* † It is therefore necessary that God come to the rescue, and that, mindful of His mercy, He turn an eye of compassion on human society. Hence, We renew the urgent entreaty We have already made, to redouble zeal and perseverance, when addressing humble supplications to our merciful God, so that the virtues whereby a Christian life is perfected may be re-awakened. It is,

<small>The evils threatening nations are the punishment of decay of faith and morals.</small>

---

* *Prov.* xiv. 34. † *Is.* v. 20.

Charity must be restored, towards God and our neighbour. however, urgent before all, that charity, which is the main foundation of the Christian life, and apart from which the other virtues exist not or remain barren, should be quickened and maintained. Therefore is it that the Apostle St. Paul, after having exhorted the Colossians to flee all vice and cultivate all virtue, adds: *Above all things have charity, which is the bond of perfection.** Yea, truly, charity is the bond of perfection, for it binds intimately to God those whom it has embraced and with loving tenderness, causes them to draw their life from God, to act with God, to refer all to God. Howbeit the love of God should not be severed from the love of our neighbour, since men have a share in the infinite goodness of God and bear in themselves the impress of His image and likeness. *This commandment we have from God, that he who loveth God, love also his brother.*† *If any man say I love God, and he hateth his brother, he is a liar.*‡ And this commandment concerning charity its Divine Proclaimer styled *new*, not in the sense that a previous law, or even nature itself, had not enjoined that men should love one another, but because the

Love of our neighbour carefully preserved amongst the early Christians.

Christian precept of loving each other in that manner was truly new, and quite unheard of in the memory of man. For that love with which Jesus Christ is beloved by His Father and with which He Himself loves men, He obtained for His disciples and followers, that they might

---

* *Coloss.* iii. 14.   † 1 *John* iv. 21.   ‡ *Ibid.* iv. 20.

be of one heart and of one mind in Him by charity, as He Himself and His Father are one by their nature. No one is unaware how deeply and from the very beginning that precept has been implanted in the breast of Christians, and what abundant fruits of concord, mutual benevolence, piety, patience, and fortitude it has produced. Why then should we not devote ourselves to imitate the examples set by our fathers? The very times in which we live, should afford sufficient motives for the practice of charity. Since impious men are bent on giving fresh impulse to their hatred against Jesus Christ, Christians should be quickened anew in piety; and charity, which is the inspirer of lofty deeds, should be imbued with new life. Let dissensions therefore, if there be any, wholly cease; let those strifes which waste the strength of those engaged in the fight, without any advantage resulting to religion, be scattered to the winds; let all minds be united in faith and all hearts in charity, so that, as it behoves, life may be spent in the practice of the love of God and the love of men.

How necessary it is in these our times.

Warning to parents to bring up their children as true Christians.

This is a suitable moment for Us to exhort especially heads of families to govern their households according to these precepts, and to be solicitous without failing for the right training of their children. The family may be regarded as the cradle of Civil society, and it is in great measure within the circle of family life that the destiny of the State is fostered. Whence it is that they who would break away from Christian discipline are working to corrupt family life, and to destroy it utterly, root and branch. From such an unholy purpose they allow not themselves to be turned aside by the reflection that it cannot, even in any degree, be carried out without inflicting cruel outrage on the parents. These hold from nature their right of training the children to whom they have given birth, with the obligation superadded of shaping and directing the education of their little ones to the end for which God vouchsafed the privilege of transmitting the gift of life. It is then incumbent on parents to strain every nerve to ward off such an outrage, and to strive manfully to have and to hold exclusive authority to direct the education of their offspring, as is fitting, in a Christian manner; and first and foremost to keep them away from schools where there is risk of their drinking in the poison of impiety. Where the right education of youth is concerned, no amount of trouble or labour can be undertaken, how great soever, but that even greater still may not be called for. In this regard indeed there are to be found in many countries Catholics worthy of general admiration, who incur considerable outlay and bestow much zeal in founding schools for the education of youth. It is highly desirable that such noble example may be generously followed, where time and circumstances demand; yet all should be intimately persuaded that the minds of children are most influenced by the training they receive at home. If in their early years they find within the walls of their homes the rule of an upright life and the discipline of Christian

The nature of Christian training.

Commendation of Catholics who have defrayed the expenses of schools.

CHRISTIANS AS CITIZENS. 137

virtues, the future welfare of the State will in great measure be guaranteed.

And now We seem to have touched upon those matters which Catholics ought chiefly now-a-days to follow, or mainly to avoid. It rests then with you, Venerable Brothers, to take measures that Our voice may reach everywhere, and that one and all may understand how urgent it is to reduce to practice the teachings set forth in this Our Letter. The observance of these duties cannot be troublesome or onerous, for the yoke of Jesus Christ is sweet, and His burden is light. If anything however appear too difficult of accomplishment, you will afford aid by the authority of your example, so that each one of the faithful may make more strenuous endeavour, and display a soul unconquered by difficulties. Bring it home to their minds, as We have ourselves oftentimes conveyed the warning, that matters of the highest moment and worthy of all honour are at stake, for the safeguarding of which every most toilsome effort should be readily endured; and that a sublime reward is in store for the labours of a Christian life. On the other hand, to refrain from doing battle for Jesus Christ, amounts to fighting against Him: He Himself assures us *He will deny before His Father in Heaven, those who shall have refused to confess Him on earth.* * As for Ourselves and you all, never assuredly, so long as life lasts, shall We allow Our authority, Our counsels, and Our solicitude to be in any wise lacking in the conflict. Nor is it to be doubted but that especial aid of the great God will be vouchsafed,

The clergy should exert all their zeal.

---
* *Luke* ix. 26.

so long as the struggle endures, to the flock alike and to the Pastors.

Sustained by this confidence, as a pledge of heavenly gifts, and of Our loving-kindness in the Lord to you, Venerable Brothers, to your clergy and to all your people, We accord the Apostolic Benediction.

HUMAN LIBERTY.

(Encyclical Letter, June 20, 1888.)

By Liberty man is master of his actions.

LIBERTY, the highest of natural endowment, being the portion only of intellectual or rational natures, confers on man this dignity —that he is *in the hand of his counsel* and has power over his actions. But the manner in which such dignity is exercised is of the greatest moment, inasmuch as on the use that is made of Liberty the highest good and the greatest evil alike depend. Man, indeed, is free to obey his reason, to seek moral good, and to strive unswervingly after his last end. Yet he is free also to turn aside to all other things, and, in pursuing the empty semblance of good, to disturb rightful order and to fall headlong into the destruction which he has voluntarily chosen. The Redeemer of mankind, Jesus Christ, having restored and exalted the original dignity of nature, vouchsafed special assistance to the will of man; and by the gifts of His grace here, and the promise of heavenly bliss hereafter, He raised it to a nobler state. In like manner this great gift of nature has ever been, and always will be, deservingly cherished by the Catholic Church; for to her alone has been committed the charge of handing down to all ages the benefits

Importance of using it aright.

What religion has done for Liberty.

purchased for us by Jesus Christ. Yet there are many who imagine that the Church is hostile to human liberty. Having a false and absurd notion as to what liberty is, either they pervert the very idea of freedom, or they extend it at their pleasure to many things in respect of which man cannot rightly be regarded as free.

Modern notions of Liberty. We have on other occasions, and especially in Our Encyclical Letter *Immortale Dei*, in treating of the so-called *modern liberties*, distinguished between their good and evil elements; and We have shown that whatsoever is good in those liberties is as ancient as truth itself, and that the Church has always most willingly approved and practised that good: but whatsoever has been added as new is, to tell the plain truth, of a vitiated kind, the fruit of the disorders of the age and of an insatiate longing after novelties. Seeing, however, that many cling so obstinately to their own opinion in this matter as to imagine these modern liberties, cankered as they are, to be the greatest glory of our age, and the very basis of civil life, without which no perfect government can be conceived, We feel it a pressing duty, for the sake of the common good, to treat separately of this subject.

Christian aspect of Liberty.—1. Natural Liberty. It is with *moral* liberty, whether in individuals or in communities, that We proceed at once to deal.

But, first of all, it will be well to speak briefly of *natural* liberty: for, though it is distinct and separate from moral liberty, natural freedom is the fountain-head from which liberty of whatsoever kind flows, *sua vi suaque sponte.* The unanimous consent and judgment of men, which is the trusty voice of nature, recognises this natural liberty in those only who are endowed with intelligence or reason; and it is by his use of this that man is rightly regarded as responsible for his actions. For, while other animate creatures follow their senses, seeking good and avoiding evil only by instinct, man has reason to guide him in each and every act of his life. Reason sees that whatever things are held to be good upon earth, may exist or may not, and discerning that none of them are of necessity for us, it leaves the will free to choose what it pleases. But man can judge of this *contingency*, as we say, only because he has a soul that is simple, spiritual, and intellectual—a soul, therefore, which is not produced by matter, and does not depend on matter for its existence; but which is created immediately by God, and, far surpassing the condition of things material, has a life and action of its own—so that, knowing the unchangeable and necessary reasons of what is true and good, it sees that no particular kind of good is necessary to us. When, therefore, it is established that man's soul is immortal and endowed with reason and not bound up with things material, the foundation of natural liberty is at once most firmly laid.

Man, being rational, is therefore free.

As the Catholic Church declares in the strongest terms the simplicity, spirituality, and immortality of the soul, so with unequalled constancy and publicity she ever also asserts its freedom. These truths she has always taught, and has sustained them as

The Church has ever upheld this freedom.

a dogma of faith; and whensoever heretics or innovators have attacked the liberty of man, the Church has defended it and protected this noble possession from destruction. History bears witness to the energy with which she met the fury of the Manicheans and others like them; and the earnestness with which in later years she defended human liberty in the Council of Trent, and against the followers of Jansenius, is known to all. At no time, and in no place, has she held truce with *fatalism*.

Its definition.

Liberty, then, as We have said, belongs only to those who have the gift of reason or intelligence. Considered as to its nature, it is the faculty of choosing means fitted for the end proposed; for he is master of his actions who can choose one thing out of many. Now, since everything chosen as a means is viewed as good or useful, and since good, as such, is the proper object of our desire, it follows that freedom of choice is a property of the will, or rather is identical with the will in so far as it has in its action the faculty of choice.

It lies in the will enlightened by reason.

But the will cannot proceed to act until it is enlightened by the knowledge possessed by the intellect. In other words, the good wished by the will is necessarily good in so far as it is known by the intellect; and this the more, because in all voluntary acts choice is subsequent to a judgment upon the truth of the good presented, declaring to which good preference should be given. No sensible man can doubt that judgment is an act of reason, not of the will. The end, or object, both of the rational will and of its liberty is that good only which is in conformity with reason.

The power of choosing evil implies defect in human freedom. Since, however, both these faculties are imperfect, it is possible, as is often seen, that the reason should propose something which is not really good, but which has the appearance of good, and that the will should choose accordingly. For, as the possibility of error, and actual error, are defects of the mind and attest its imperfection, so the pursuit of what has a false appearance of good, though a proof of our freedom, just as a disease is a proof of our vitality, implies defect in human liberty. The will also, simply because of its dependence on the reason, no sooner desires anything contrary thereto, than it abuses its freedom of choice and corrupts its very essence. Thus it is that the infinitely perfect God, although supremely free, because of the supremacy of His intellect and of His essential goodness, nevertheless cannot choose evil; neither can the Angels and Saints, who enjoy the Beatific Vision. St. Augustine and others urged most admirably against the Pelagians, that, if the possibility of deflection from good belonged to the essence or perfection of liberty, then God, Jesus Christ, and the Angels and Saints, who have not this power, would have no liberty at all, or would have less liberty than man has in his state of pilgrimage and imperfection. This subject is often discussed by the Angelic Doctor in his demonstration that the possibility of sinning is not freedom, but slavery. It will suffice to quote his subtle commentary on the words of our Lord: *Whosoever* *committeth sin is the slave of sin.** "Everything," he says, "is that which belongs to it naturally. When, therefore, it acts through a power outside itself, it does not act of itself, but through another, that is, as a slave. But man is by nature rational. When, therefore, he acts according to reason, he acts of himself and according to his free-will; and this is liberty. Whereas, when he sins, he acts in opposition to reason, is moved by another, and is the victim of foreign misapprehensions. Therefore, *Whosoever committeth sin is the slave of sin.*" Even the heathen philosophers clearly recognised this truth, especially they who held that the wise man alone is free; and by the term "wise man" was meant, as is well known, the man trained to live in accordance with his nature, that is, in justice and virtue.

2.—Moral Liberty.

Such then being the condition of human liberty, it necessarily stands in need of light and strength to direct its actions to good and to restrain them from evil. Without this the freedom of our will would be our ruin. First of all

Necessity of law.

there must be *law;* that is, a fixed rule of teaching what is to be done and what is to be left undone. This rule cannot affect the lower animals in any true sense, since they act of necessity, following their natural instinct, and cannot of themselves act in any other way. On the other hand, as was said above, he who is free can either act or not act, can do this or do that, as he pleases, because his judgment precedes his choice. And his judgment not only decides what is right or wrong of its own nature,

---

* *John* viii. 34.

but also what is practically good and therefore to be chosen, and what is practically evil and therefore to be avoided. In other words the reason prescribes to the will what it should seek after or shun, in order to the eventual attainment of man's last end, for the sake of which all his actions ought to be performed. This ordination of *reason* is called law. In man's free-will, therefore, or in the moral necessity of our voluntary acts being in accordance with reason, lies the very root of the necessity of law. Nothing more foolish can be uttered or conceived than the notion that because man is free by nature, he is therefore exempt from law. Were this the case, it would follow that to become free we must be deprived of reason; whereas the truth is that we are bound to submit to law precisely because we are free by our very nature. For law is the guide of man's actions; it turns him towards good by its rewards, and deters him from evil by its punishments.

<small>Natural law, which is our reason commanding us to do good and avoid evil.</small>

Foremost in this office comes the *natural law*, which is written and engraved in the mind of every man; and this is nothing but our reason, commanding us to do right and forbidding sin. Nevertheless all prescriptions of human reason can have force of law only inasmuch as they are the voice and the interpreters of some higher power on which our reason and liberty necessarily depend. For, since the force of law consists in the imposing of obligations and the granting of rights, authority is the one and only foundation of all law—the power, that is, of fixing duties and defining rights, as also of assigning the

K

necessary sanctions of reward and chastisement to each and all of its commands. But all this, clearly, cannot be found in man, if, as his own supreme legislator, he is to be the rule of his own actions. It follows therefore that the law of nature is the same thing as the *eternal law*, implanted in rational creatures, and inclining them *to their right action and end;* and can be nothing else but the eternal reason of God, the Creator and Ruler of all the world. To this rule of action and restraint of evil God has vouchsafed to give special and most suitable aids for strengthening and ordering the human will. The first and most excellent of these is the power of His divine *grace*, whereby the mind can be enlightened and the will wholesomely invigorated and moved to the constant pursuit of moral good, so that the use of our in-born liberty becomes at once less difficult and less dangerous. Not that the Divine assistance hinders in any way the free movement of our will; just the contrary, for grace works inwardly in man and in harmony with his natural inclinations, since it flows from the very Creator of his mind and will, by Whom all things are moved in conformity with their nature. As the Angelic Doctor points out, it is because divine grace comes from the Author of nature, that it is so admirably adapted to be the safeguard of all natures, and to maintain the character, efficiency, and operations of each.

What has been said of the liberty of individuals is no

less applicable to them when considered as bound together in civil society. For, what reason and the natural law do for individuals, that *human law*, promulgated for their good, does for the citizens of States. Of the laws enacted by men, some are concerned with what is good or bad by its very nature; and they command men to follow after what is right and to shun what is wrong, adding at the same time a suitable sanction. But such laws by no means derive their origin from civil society; because, just as civil society did not create human nature, so neither can it be said to be the author of the good which befits human nature, or of the evil which is contrary to it. Laws come before men live together in society, and have their origin in the natural, and consequently in the eternal, law. The precepts, therefore, of the natural law, contained bodily in the laws of men, have not merely the force of human law, but they possess that higher and more august sanction which belongs to the law of nature and the eternal law. And within the sphere of this kind of laws, the duty of the civil legislator is, mainly, to keep the community in obedience by the adoption of a common discipline and by putting restraint upon refractory and viciously inclined men, so that, deterred from evil, they may turn to what is good, or at any rate may avoid causing trouble and disturbance to the State. Now there are other enactments of the Civil authority, which do not follow directly, but somewhat remotely, from the natural

(marginal notes: Human law; enforces the natural law, and applies its general precepts to particular cases.)

law, and decide many points which the law of nature treats only in a general and indefinite way. For instance, though nature commands all to contribute to the public peace and prosperity, still whatever belongs to the manner, and circumstances, and conditions under which such service is to be rendered must be determined by the wisdom of men, and not by nature herself. It is in the constitution of these particular rules of life, suggested by reason and prudence, and put forth by competent authority, that human law, properly so called, consists, binding all citizens to work together for the attainment of the common end proposed to the community, and forbidding them to depart from this end; and in so far as human law is in conformity with the dictates of nature, leading to what is good, and deterring from evil.

Hence the eternal law is the standard of true liberty.

From this it is manifest that the eternal law of God is the sole standard and rule of human liberty, not only in each individual man, but also in the community and civil society which men constitute when united. Therefore, the true liberty of human society does not consist in every man doing what he pleases, for this would simply end in turmoil and confusion, and bring on the overthrow of the State; but rather in this, that through the injunctions of the civil law all may more easily conform to the prescriptions of the eternal law. Likewise, the liberty of those who are in authority does not consist in the power to lay unreasonable and capricious commands upon their subjects, which would equally be criminal and would lead to the ruin of the commonwealth; but the binding force of human laws is in this, that they are to be regarded as applications of the eternal law, and incapable of sanctioning anything which is not contained in the eternal law, as in the principle of all law. Thus St. Augustine most wisely says: "I think that you can see, at the same time, that there is nothing just and lawful in that temporal law, unless what men have gathered from this eternal law."* If, then, by any one in authority, something be sanctioned out of conformity with the principles of right reason, and consequently hurtful to the commonwealth, such an enactment can have no binding force of law, as being no rule of justice, but certain to lead men away from that good which is the very end of civil society.

Therefore, the nature of human liberty, however it be considered, whether in individuals or in society, whether in those who command or in those who obey, supposes the necessity of obedience to some supreme and eternal law, which is no other than the authority of God, commanding good and forbidding evil. And, so far from this most just authority of God over men diminishing, or even destroying their liberty, it protects and perfects it; for the real perfection of all creatures is found in the prosecution and attainment of their respective ends; but the supreme end to which human liberty must aspire is God.

The Church has ever promoted true freedom, These precepts of the truest and highest teaching, made known to us by the light of reason itself, the Church, instructed by the example and

---

De Libero Arbitrio, lib. i. cap. 6, n. 15.

doctrine of her Divine Author, has ever propagated and asserted: for she has ever made them the measure of her office and of her teaching to the Christian nations. As to morals, the laws of the Gospel not only immeasurably surpass the wisdom of the heathen, but are an invitation and an introduction to a state of holiness unknown to the ancients; and, bringing man nearer to God, they make him at once the possessor of a more perfect liberty. Thus the powerful influence of the Church has ever been manifested in the custody and protection of the civil and political liberty of the people.

by abolishing slavery and by spreading civilisation;

The enumeration of its merits in this respect does not belong to our present purpose. It is sufficient to recall the fact that slavery, that old reproach of the heathen nations, was mainly abolished by the beneficent efforts of the Church. The impartiality of law and the true brotherhood of man were first asserted by Jesus Christ; and His Apostles re-echoed His voice, when they declared that in future there was to be neither Jew, nor Gentile, nor barbarian, nor Scythian, but all were brothers in Christ. So powerful, so conspicuous in this respect, is the influence of the Church, that experience abundantly testifies how savage customs are no longer possible in any land where she has once set her foot; but that gentleness speedily takes the place of cruelty, and the light of truth quickly dispels the darkness of barbarism. Nor has the Church been less lavish in the benefits she has conferred on civilised nations in every age, either by resisting the tyranny of the wicked, or by protecting the innocent and helpless from injury; or finally by using her influence in the support of any form of government which commended itself to the citizens at home, because of its justice, or was feared by their enemies without, because of its power.

by inculcating respect and obedience to lawful authority;

Moreover, the highest duty is to respect authority, and obediently to submit to just law; and by this the members of a community are effectually protected from the wrong-doing of evil men. Lawful power is from God, *and whosoever resisteth authority resisteth the ordinance of God;* wherefore, obedience is greatly ennobled, when subjected to an authority which is the most just and supreme of all. But where

by laying down the limits of human authority.

the power to command is wanting, or where a law is enacted contrary to reason, or to the eternal law, or to some ordinance of God, obedience is unlawful, lest, while obeying man, we become disobedient to God. Thus, an effectual barrier being opposed to tyranny, the authority in the State will not have all its own way, but the interests and rights of all will be safeguarded—the rights of individuals, of domestic society, and of all the members of the commonwealth; all being free to live according to law and right reason; and in this, as We have shown, true liberty really consists.

Liberalism

If when men discuss the question of liberty, they were careful to grasp its true and legitimate meaning, such as reason and reasoning have just explained, they would never venture to affix such a calumny on the Church as to assert that she is the foe to individual and public liberty. But many there are who follow in the footsteps of Lucifer, and adopt as their own his rebellious cry, "I will not serve;" and consequently substitute for true liberty what is sheer and most foolish licence. Such, for instance, are the men belonging to that widely-spread and powerful organisation, who, usurping the name of liberty, style themselves *Liberals*.

What *Naturalists* or *Rationalists* aim at in philosophy, that the supporters of *Liberalism*, carrying out the principles laid down by Naturalism, are attempting in the domain of morality and politics. The fundamental doctrine of *Rationalism* is the supremacy of the human reason, which, refusing due submission to the divine and eternal reason, proclaims its own independence, and constitutes itself the supreme principle and source and judge of truth. Hence these followers of Liberalism deny the existence of any divine authority to which obedience is due, and proclaim that every man is the law to himself; from which arises that ethical system which they style *independent* morality, and which, under the guise of liberty, exonerates man from any obedience to the commands of God, and substitutes a boundless licence. The end of all this it is not difficult to foresee, especially when Society is in question. For, when once man is firmly persuaded that he is subject to no one, it follows that the efficient cause of the unity of civil society is not to be sought, in any principle external to man, or superior to him, but simply in the free-will of individuals; that the authority in the State comes from the people only;

casts aside divine authority.

Its logical issue.

and that, just as every man's individual reason is his only rule of life, so the collective reason of the community should be the supreme guide in the management of all public affairs. Hence the doctrine of the supremacy of the greater number, and that all right and all duty reside in the majority. But, from what has been said, it is clear that all this is in contradiction to reason.

<small>which is repugnant to reason.</small>

To refuse any bond of union between man and civil society, on the one hand, and God, the Creator and consequently the supreme Law-Giver, on the other, is plainly repugnant to the nature, not only of man, but of all created things: for, of necessity, all effects must in some proper way be connected with their cause; and it belongs to the perfection of every nature to contain itself within that sphere and grade which the order of nature has assigned to it; namely, that the lower should be subject and obedient to the higher.

Moreover, besides this, a doctrine of such a character is most hurtful both to individuals and to the State.

<small>Its dangerous consequences.</small>

For, once ascribe to human reason the only authority to decide what is true and what is good, and the real distinction between good and evil is destroyed; honour and dishonour differ not in their nature, but in the opinion and judgment of each one; pleasure is the measure of what is lawful; and, given a code of morality which can have little or no power to restrain or quiet the unruly propensities of man, a way is naturally opened to universal corruption. With reference also to public affairs: authority is severed from the true and natural principle whence it derives all its efficacy for the common good; and the law determining what it is right to do and avoid doing is at the mercy of a majority. Now this is simply a road leading straight to tyranny. The empire of God over man and civil society once repudiated, it follows that religion, as a public institution, can have no claim to exist, and that everything that belongs to religion will be treated with complete indifference. Furthermore, with ambitious designs on sovereignty, tumult and sedition will be common amongst the people; and when duty and conscience cease to appeal to them, there will be nothing to hold them back but force, which of itself alone is powerless to keep their covetousness in check. Of this we have almost daily evidence in the conflict with *Socialists* and members of other seditious societies, who labour unceasingly to bring about revolution. It is for those, then, who are capable of forming a just estimate of things, to decide whether such doctrines promote that true liberty which alone is worthy of man, or rather pervert and destroy it.

Another form of Liberalism limits obedience by the natural law.
There are, indeed, some adherents of Liberalism who do not subscribe to these opinions, which we have seen to be fearful in their enormity, openly opposed to the truth, and the cause of most terrible evils. Indeed, very many amongst them, compelled by the force of truth, do not hesitate to admit that such liberty is vicious, nay is simple licence, whenever intemperate in its claims, to the neglect of truth and justice; and therefore they would have liberty

ruled and directed by right reason, and consequently subject to the natural law and to the divine eternal law. But here they think they may stop, holding that man as a free being is bound by no law of God, except such as He makes known to us through our natural reason.

Its inconsistency. In this they are plainly inconsistent. For if—as they must admit, and no one can rightly deny, the will of the Divine Law-Giver is to be obeyed,—because every man is under the power of God, and tends towards Him as his end—it follows that no one can assign limits to His legislative authority without failing in the obedience which is due. Indeed, if the human mind be so presumptuous as to define the nature and extent of God's rights and its own duties, reverence for the divine law will be apparent rather than real, and arbitrary judgment will prevail over the authority and providence of God. Man must, therefore, take his standard of a loyal and religious life from the eternal law; and from all and every one of those laws which God, in His infinite wisdom and power, has been pleased to enact, and to make known to us by such clear and unmistakable signs as to leave no room for doubt. And the more so, because laws of this kind have the same origin, the same author, as the eternal law, are absolutely in accordance with right reason, and perfect the natural law. These laws it is that embody the government of God, Who graciously guides and directs both the intellect and the will of man lest these fall into error. Let, then, that continue to remain in a holy and inviolable union, which neither can nor should, be separated; and in all things—for this is the dictate of right reason itself—let God be dutifully and obediently served.

<small>Another form holds that individuals are subject to the Divine law, but not the State.</small>

There are others, somewhat more moderate though not more consistent, who affirm that the morality of individuals is to be guided by the divine law, but not the morality of the State, so that in public affairs the commands of God may be passed over, and may be entirely disregarded in the framing of laws. Hence follows the fatal theory of the need of separation between Church and State. But

<small>This view is inconsistent with the end of the State.</small>

the absurdity of such a position is manifest. Nature herself proclaims the necessity of the State providing means and opportunities whereby the community may be enabled to live properly, that is to say, according to the laws of God. For, since God is the source of all goodness and justice, it is absolutely ridiculous that the State should pay no attention to these laws or render them abortive by contrary enactments. Besides, those who are in authority owe it to the commonwealth not only to provide for its external well-being and the conveniences of life, but still more to consult the welfare of men's souls in the wisdom of their legislation. But, for the increase of such benefits, nothing more suitable can be conceived than the laws which have God for their author; and, therefore, they who in their government of the State take no account of these laws, abuse political power by causing it to deviate from its proper end and from what nature itself prescribes. And, what is still more important, and what We have more than once pointed out, although the Civil authority has not the same proximate end as the spiritual, nor proceeds on the same lines, nevertheless in the exercise of their separate powers they must occasionally meet. For their subjects are the same : and not unfrequently they deal with the same objects, though in different ways. Whenever this occurs, since a state of conflict is absurd and manifestly repugnant to the most wise ordinance of God, there must necessarily exist some order or mode of procedure to remove the occasions of difference and contention, and to secure harmony in all things. This harmony has been not inaptly compared to that which exists between the body and the soul, for the well-being of both one and the other; the separation of which brings irremediable harm to the body, since it extinguishes its very life.

<small>Some false doctrines of Liberalism, —Liberty of worship.</small>
To make this more evident, the growth of liberty ascribed to our age must be considered apart in its various details. And, first, let us examine that liberty in individuals which is so opposed to the virtue of religion, namely, the *liberty of worship*, as it is called. This is based on the principle that every man is free to profess as he may choose any religion or none.

<small>Man must worship God in the way God wills.</small>
But, assuredly, of all the duties which man has to fulfil, that, without doubt, is the chiefest and holiest which commands him to worship God with devotion and piety. This follows of necessity from the truth that we are ever in the power of God, are ever guided by His will and providence, and, having come forth from

Him, must return to Him. Add to which, no true virtue can exist without religion: for moral virtue is concerned with those things which lead to God as man's supreme and ultimate good: and therefore religion, which (as St. Thomas says) "performs those actions which are directly and immediately ordained for the divine honour,"* rules and tempers all virtues. And if it be asked which of the many conflicting religions it is necessary to adopt, reason and the natural law unhesitatingly tell us to practise that one which God enjoins, and which men can easily recognise by certain exterior notes, whereby Divine Providence has willed that it should be distinguished, because, in a matter of such moment, the most terrible loss would be the consequence of error. Wherefore, when a liberty such as we have described, is offered to man, the power is given him to pervert or abandon with impunity the most sacred of duties, and to exchange the unchangeable good for evil; which, as we have said, is no liberty, but its degradation, and the abject submission of the soul to sin.

in the one true religion.

The State also is bound to worship God in a form acceptable to Him.

This kind of liberty, if considered in relation to the State, clearly implies that there is no reason why the State should offer any homage to God, or should desire any public recognition of Him; that no one form of worship is to be preferred to another, but that all stand on an equal footing: no account being taken of the religion of

---

* *Summa*, 2a 2æ, q. lxxxi. a. 6.

the people, even if they profess the Catholic faith. But, to justify this, it must needs be taken as true that the State has no duties towards God, or that such duties, if they exist, can be abandoned with impunity; both of which assertions are manifestly false. For it cannot be doubted but that, by the will of God, men are united in civil society; whether its component parts be considered; or its form, which implies authority; or the object of its existence; or the abundance of the vast services which it renders to man. God it is Who has made man for society, and has placed him in the company of others like himself, so that what was wanting to his nature, and beyond his attainment if left to his own resources, he might obtain by association with others. Wherefore civil society must acknowledge God as its Founder and Parent, and must obey and reverence His power and authority. Justice therefore forbids, and reason itself forbids, the State to be godless; or to adopt a line of action which would end in godlessness,—namely, to treat the various religions (as they call them) alike, and to bestow upon them promiscuously equal rights and privileges. Since, then, the profession of one religion is necessary in the State, that religion must be professed which alone is true, and which can be recognised without difficulty, especially in Catholic States, because the marks of truth are, as it were, engraven upon it. This religion, therefore, the rulers of the State must preserve and protect, if they would provide—as they should do—with prudence and usefulness for the good of the community. For public authority exists for the welfare of those whom it governs; and although its proximate end is to lead men to the prosperity found in this life, yet, in so doing, it ought not to diminish, but rather to increase, man's capability of attaining to the supreme good in which his everlasting happiness consists: which never can be attained if religion be disregarded.

The public profession of Religion is helpful to the liberty of rulers and ruled.

All this, however, We have explained more fully elsewhere. We now only wish to add the remark that liberty of so false a nature is greatly hurtful to the true liberty of both rulers and their subjects. Religion, of its essence, is wonderfully helpful to the State. For, since it derives the prime origin of all all power directly from God Himself, with grave authority it charges rulers to be mindful of their duty, to govern without injustice or severity, to rule their people kindly and with almost paternal charity; it admonishes subjects to be obedient to lawful authority, as to the ministers of God; and it binds them to their rulers, not merely by obedience, but by reverence and affection, forbidding all seditions and venturesome enterprises calculated to disturb public order and tranquillity, and cause greater restrictions to be put upon the liberty of the people. We need not mention how greatly religion conduces to pure morals, and pure morals to liberty. Reason shows, and history confirms the fact, that the higher the morality of States, the greater are the liberty and wealth and power which they enjoy.

Liberty of the Press supposes a right to circulate falsehood.

We must now consider briefly *liberty of speech*, and liberty of the Press. It is hardly necessary to say that there can be no such right as this, if it be not used in moderation, and if it pass beyond the bounds and end of all true liberty. For right is a moral power which—as We have before said and must again and again repeat—it is absurd to suppose that nature has accorded indifferently to truth and falsehood, to justice and injustice. Men have a right freely and prudently to propagate throughout the State what things soever are true and honourable, so that as many as possible may possess them; but lying opinions, than which no mental plague is greater, and vices which corrupt the heart and moral life, should be diligently repressed by public authority, lest they insidiously work the ruin of the State. The excesses of an unbridled intellect, which unfailingly end in the oppression of the untutored multitude, are no less rightly controlled by the authority of the law than are the injuries inflicted by violence upon the weak. And this all the more surely, because by far the greater part of the community is either absolutely unable, or able only with great difficulty, to escape from illusions and deceitful subtleties, especially such as flatter the passions. If unbridled licence of speech and of writing be granted to all, nothing will remain sacred and inviolate; even the highest and truest mandates of nature, justly held to be the common and noblest heritage of the human race, will not be spared. Thus, truth being gradually obscured by darkness, pernicious and manifold error, as too often happens, will easily prevail. Thus, too, licence will gain what liberty loses; for liberty will ever be more free and secure, in proportion as licence is kept in fuller restraint. In regard however to all matters of opinion which God leaves

L

to man's free discussion, full liberty of thought and of speech is naturally within the right of every one; for such liberty never leads men to suppress the truth, but often to discover it and make it known.

Truth being the perfection of the intellect can alone be lawfully taught.

A like judgment must be passed upon what is called *liberty of teaching*. There can be no doubt that truth alone should imbue the minds of men; for in it are found the well-being, the end, and the perfection of every intelligent nature: and therefore nothing but truth should be taught both to the ignorant and to the educated, so as to bring knowledge to those who have it not, and to preserve it in those who possess it. For this reason it is plainly the duty of all who teach to banish error from the mind, and by sure safeguards to close the entry to all false convictions. From this it follows, as is evident, that the liberty of which We have been speaking, is greatly opposed to reason, and tends absolutely to pervert men's minds, in as much as it claims for itself the right of teaching whatever it pleases—a liberty which the State cannot grant without failing in its duty. And the more so, because the authority of teachers has great weight with their hearers, who can rarely decide for themselves as to the truth or falsehood of the instruction given to them.

Natural and supernatural truth cannot be mutually opposed.

Wherefore, this liberty also, in order that it may deserve the name, must be kept within certain limits, lest the office of teaching be turned with impunity into an instrument of corruption. Now truth, which should be the only subject-matter of those who teach, is of two kinds, natural and supernatural. Of natural truths, such as the principles of nature and whatever is derived from them immediately by our reason, there is a kind of common patrimony in the human race. On this, as on a firm basis, morality, justice, religion, and the very bonds of human society rest: and to allow people to go unharmed who violate or destroy it, would be most impious, most foolish, and most inhuman. But with no less religious care must we preserve that great and sacred treasure of the truths which God Himself has taught us. By many and convincing arguments, often used by defenders of Christianity, certain leading truths have been laid down: namely, that some things have been revealed by God; that the Only-Begotten Son of God was made Flesh, to bear witness to the truth; that a perfect Society was founded by Him—the Church namely, of which He is the Head, and with which He has promised to abide till the end of the world. To this Society He entrusted all the truths which He had taught, in order that it might keep and guard them and with lawful authority explain them; and at the same time He commanded all nations to hear the voice of the Church, as if it were His own, threatening those who would not hear it with everlasting perdition. Thus it is manifest that man's best and surest teacher is God, the source and principle of all truth; and the Only-Begotten Son, Who is in the bosom of the Father, the Way, the Truth, and the Life, the true Light which enlightens every man, and to Whose teaching all must submit: *And they shall all be taught of God.* * In faith and in the teaching of

---

* *John* vi. 45.

morality, God Himself made the Church a partaker of His divine authority, and through His heavenly gift she cannot be deceived. She is therefore the greatest and most reliable teacher of mankind, and in her dwells an inviolable right to teach them. Sustained by the truth received from her Divine Founder, the Church has ever sought to fulfil holily the mission entrusted to her by God; unconquered by the difficulties on all sides surrounding her, she has never ceased to assert her liberty of teaching; and in this way, the wretched superstition of Paganism being dispelled, the wide world was renewed unto Christian wisdom. Now, reason itself clearly teaches that the truths of divine revelation and those of nature cannot really be opposed to one another, and that whatever is at variance with them must necessarily be false. Therefore the divine teaching of the Church, so far from being an obstacle to the pursuit of learning and the progress of science, or in any way retarding the advance of civilisation, in reality brings to them the sure guidance of shining light. And for the same reason it is of no small advantage for the perfecting of human liberty; since our Saviour Jesus Christ has said that by truth is man made free: *You shall know the truth, and the truth shall make you free.* * Therefore, there is no reason why genuine liberty should grow indignant, or true science feel aggrieved, at having to bear the just and necessary restraint of laws, by which, in the judgment of the Church and of reason itself, human teaching has to be controlled. The Church, indeed,—as facts have

The teaching of the Church is beneficial to science;

---
* *John* viii. 32.

everywhere proved—looks chiefly and above all to the defence of the Christian faith, while careful at the same time to foster and promote every kind of human learning. For learning is in itself good, and praiseworthy, and desirable; and further all erudition which is the outgrowth of sound reason, and in conformity with the truth of things, serves not a little to confirm what we believe on the authority of God. The Church, truly, to our great benefit, has carefully preserved the monuments of ancient wisdom; has opened everywhere homes of science; and has urged on intellectual progress, by fostering most diligently the arts by which the culture of our age is so much advanced. Lastly, We must not forget that a vast field lies freely open to man's industry and genius, containing all those things which have no necessary connection with Christian faith and morals, or as to which the Church, exercising no authority, leaves the judgment of the learned free and unconstrained. From all this may be understood the nature and character of that liberty which the followers of *Liberalism* so eagerly advocate and proclaim. On the one hand, they demand for themselves and for the State a licence which opens the way to every perversity of opinion; and on the other, they hamper the Church in divers ways, restricting her liberty within narrowest limits, although from her teaching not only is there nothing to be feared, but in every respect very much to be gained.

and is a safeguard of true freedom.

Another liberty is widely advocated, namely, *liberty of conscience.* If by this is meant that everyone may,

True and false Liberty of Conscience.

as he chooses, worship God or not, it is sufficiently refuted by the arguments already adduced. But it may also be taken to mean that every man in the State may follow the will of God and, from a consciousness of duty and free from every obstacle, obey His commands. This, indeed, is true liberty, a liberty worthy of the sons of God, which nobly maintains the dignity of man, and is stronger than all violence or wrong—a liberty which the Church has always desired and held most dear. This is the kind of liberty the Apostles claimed for themselves with intrepid constancy, which the Apologists of Christianity confirmed by their writings, and which the Martyrs in vast numbers consecrated by their blood. And deservedly so; for this Christian liberty bears witness to the absolute and most just dominion of God over man, and to the chief and supreme duty of man towards God. It has nothing in common with a seditious and rebellious mind; and in no tittle derogates from obedience to public authority : for the right to command and to require obedience exists only so far as it is in accordance with the authority of God, and is within the measure that He has laid down. But when anything is commanded which is plainly at variance with the will of God, there is a wide departure from this divinely constituted order, and at the same time a direct conflict with Divine Authority; therefore it is right not to obey.

By the patrons of *Liberalism*, however, who make the State absolute and omnipotent, and proclaim that man should live altogether independently of God, the liberty of which We speak, which goes hand in hand with virtue and religion, is not admitted; and whatever is done for its preservation is accounted an injury and an offence against the State. Indeed, if what they say were really true, there would be no tyranny, no matter how monstrous, which we should not be bound to endure and submit to.

The Church tolerates wrongful teaching for grave reasons. The Church most earnestly desires that the Christian teaching, of which We have given an outline, should penetrate every rank of society in reality and in practice. For it would be of the greatest efficacy in healing the evils of our day, which are neither few nor slight, and are the offspring in great part of the false liberty which is so much extolled, and in which the germs of safety and glory were supposed to be contained. The hope has been disappointed by the result. The fruit, instead of being sweet and wholesome, has proved cankered and bitter. If then a remedy is desired, let it be sought for in a restoration of sound doctrine, from which alone the preservation of order and, as a consequence, the defence of true liberty can be confidently expected. Yet, with the discernment of a true mother, the Church weighs the great burden of human weakness; and well knows the course down which the minds and actions of men are in this our age being borne. For this reason, while not conceding any right to anything save what is true and honest, she does not forbid public authority to tolerate what is at variance with truth and justice, for the sake of avoiding some greater evil, or of obtaining or preserving some greater good. God

Himself, in His providence, though infinitely good and powerful, permits evil to exist in the world, partly that greater good may not be impeded, and partly that greater evil may not ensue. In the government of States it is not forbidden to imitate the Ruler of the world; and, as the authority of man is powerless to prevent every evil, it has (as St. Augustine says) *to overlook and leave unpunished, many things which are punished, and rightly, by Divine Providence.** But if, in such circumstances, for the sake of the common good (and this is the only legitimate reason), human law may or even should tolerate evil, it may not and should not approve or desire evil for its own sake; for evil of itself, being a privation of good, is opposed to the common welfare which every legislator is bound to desire and defend to the best of his ability. In this, human law must endeavour to imitate God, Who, as St. Thomas teaches, in allowing evil to exist in the world, "*neither wills evil to be done, nor wills it not to be done, but wills only to permit it to be done; and this is good.*" † This saying of the Angelic Doctor contains briefly the whole doctrine of the permission of evil. But, to judge aright, we must acknowledge that the more a State is driven to tolerate evil the further is it from perfection; and that the tolerance of evil which is dictated by political prudence should be strictly confined to the limits which its justifying cause, the public welfare, requires. Wherefore, if such tolerance would be injurious to the public welfare, and entail greater evils on the State, it would

---

* S. August., de lib. arb., lib. 1. cap. 6, num. 14.
† S. Thomas, 1 q. xix. a 9 ad. 3.

not be lawful; for in such case the motive of good is wanting. And although in the extraordinary condition of these times, the Church usually acquiesces in certain modern liberties, not because she prefers them in themselves, but because she judges it expedient to permit them, she would in happier times exercise her own liberty; and, by persuasion, exhortation, and entreaty, would endeavour, as she is bound, to fulfil the duty assigned to her by God of providing for the eternal salvation of mankind. One thing, however, remains always true—that the liberty which is claimed for all to do all things, is not, as We have often said, of itself desirable, inasmuch as it is contrary to reason that error and truth should have equal rights. And as to *tolerance*, it is surprising how far

<small>Tolerance of evil a sign of imperfection in the State.</small> removed from the equity and prudence of the Church are those who profess what is called *Liberalism*. For, in allowing that boundless licence of which We have spoken, they exceed all limits, and end at last by making no apparent distinction between truth and error, honesty and dishonesty. And because the Church, the pillar and ground of truth, and the unerring teacher of morals, is forced utterly to reprobate and condemn *tolerance* of such an abandoned and criminal character, they calumniate her as being wanting in patience and gentleness, and thus fail to see that, in so doing, they impute to her as a fault what is in reality a matter for commendation. But, in spite of all this show of *tolerance*, it very often happens that, while they profess themselves ready to lavish liberty on all in the greatest profusion, they are utterly intolerant

towards the Catholic Church, by refusing to allow her the liberty of being herself free.

Recapitulation of the whole Letter. And now to reduce for clearness' sake to its principal heads, all that has been set forth with its immediate conclusions, the summing up is this briefly: that man, by a necessity of his nature, is wholly subject to the most faithful and ever-enduring power of God; and that as a consequence any liberty, except that which consists in submission to God and in subjection to His Will, is unintelligible. To deny the existence of this authority in God, or to refuse to submit to it, means to act, not as a free man, but as one who treasonably abuses his liberty; and in such a disposition of mind the chief and deadly vice of *Liberalism* essentially consists. The form, however, of the sin is manifold; for in more ways and degrees than one can the will depart from the obedience which is due to God or to those who share the divine power.

Various kinds and degrees of Liberalism. For, to reject the supreme authority of God, and to cast off all obedience to Him in public matters, or even in private and domestic affairs, is the greatest perversion of liberty and the worst kind of *Liberalism;* and what We have said must be understood to apply to this alone, in its fullest sense.

Next comes the system of those who admit indeed the duty of submitting to God, the Creator and Ruler of the world, inasmuch as all nature is dependent on His Will, but who boldly reject all laws of faith and morals which are above natural reason, but are revealed by the authority of God; or who at least impudently assert that there is no reason why regard should be paid to these laws, at any rate publicly, by the State. How mistaken these men also are, and how inconsistent, we have seen above. From this teaching, as from its source and principle, flows that fatal principle of the separation of Church and State; whereas it is, on the contrary, clear that the two powers, though dissimilar in functions and unequal in degree, ought nevertheless to live in concord, by harmony in their action and the faithful discharge of their respective duties.

But this teaching is understood in two ways. Many wish the State to be separated from the Church wholly and entirely, so that regard to every right of human society, in institutions, customs, and laws, the offices of State, and the education of youth, they would pay no more regard to the Church than if she did not exist; and, at most, would allow the citizens individually to attend to their religion in private if so minded. Against such as these, all the arguments by which We disprove the principle of separation of Church and State are conclusive; with this superadded, that it is absurd the citizen should respect the Church, while the State may hold her in contempt.

Rejection of the Church, or of her claims to have rights.
Others oppose not the existence of the Church, nor indeed could they; yet they despoil her of the nature and rights of a perfect society; and maintain that it does not belong to her to legislate, to judge, or to punish, but only to exhort, to advise, and to rule her subjects in accordance with their own consent

and will. By such opinion they pervert the nature of this divine Society, and attenuate and narrow its authority, its office of teacher, and its whole efficiency; and at the same time they aggrandise the power of the civil government to such extent as to subject the Church of God to the empire and sway of the State, like any voluntary association of citizens. To refute completely such teaching, the arguments often used by the defenders of Christianity, and set forth by Us, especially in the Encyclical Letter *Immortale Dei*, are of great avail; for by those arguments it is proved that, by a divine provision, all the rights which essentially belong to a society that is legitimate, supreme, and perfect in all its parts, exist in the Church.

The desire of an impossible compromise. Lastly, there remain those who, while they do not approve the separation of Church and State, think nevertheless that the Church ought to adapt herself to the times, and conform to what is required by the modern system of government. Such an opinion is sound, if it is to be understood of some equitable adjustment consistent with truth and justice; in so far, namely, that the Church, in the hope of some great good, may show herself indulgent, and may conform to the times in so far as her sacred office permits. But it is not so in regard to practices and doctrines which a perversion of morals and a warped judgment have unlawfully introduced. Religion, truth, and justice, must ever be maintained; and, as God has entrusted these great and sacred matters to the care of the Church, she can never be so unfaithful to her office as to dissemble in regard to what is false or unjust, or to connive at what is hurtful to religion.

Modern liberties, as they are called, affect dangerous independence.

From what has been said, it follows that it is quite <u>unlawful</u> to demand, to defend, or to grant, <u>unconditional</u> freedom of thought, of speech, of writing, or of worship, as if these were so many rights given by nature to man. For if nature had really granted them, it would be lawful to refuse obedience to God, and there would be no restraint on human liberty. It likewise follows, that freedom in these things may be tolerated wherever there is just cause; but only with such moderation as will prevent its degenerating into licence and excess. And where such liberties are in use, men should employ them in doing good, and should estimate them as the Church does; for liberty is to be regarded as legitimate in so far only as it affords greater facility for doing good, but no farther.

Whenever there exists, or there is reason to fear, an unjust oppression of the people on the one hand, or a deprivation of the liberty of the Church on the other, it is lawful to seek for such a change of government as will bring about due liberty of action. In such case an excessive and vicious liberty is not sought for, but only some relief, for the common welfare, in order that, while licence for evil is allowed by the State, the power of doing good may not be hindered.

Again, it is not of itself wrong to prefer a democratic form of government, if only the Catholic doctrine be maintained as to the origin and exercise of power. Of the various forms of government, the Church does not reject any that are fitted to procure the welfare of the subject; she wishes only—and this nature itself requires—that they should be constituted without involving wrong to anyone, and especially without violating the rights of the Church.

Constitutional and popular forms of Government approved by the Church.

Unless it be otherwise determined, by reason of some exceptional condition of things, it is expedient to take part in the administration of public affairs. And the Church approves of everyone devoting his services to the common good, and doing all that he can for the defence, preservation, and prosperity of his country.

Also political action for national independence.

Neither does the Church condemn those who, if it can be done without violation of justice, wish to make their country independent of any foreign or despotic power. Nor does she blame those who wish to assign to the State the power of self-government, and to its citizens the greatest possible measure of prosperity. The Church has always most faithfully fostered civil liberty, and this was seen especially in Italy, in the municipal prosperity, and wealth, and glory, which were obtained at a time when the salutary power of the Church had spread, without opposition, to all parts of the State.

These things, Venerable Brothers, which, under the guidance of faith and reason, in the discharge of Our Apostolic office, We have now delivered to you, We hope, especially by your co-operation with Us, will be useful unto very many. In lowliness of heart We raise Our eyes in supplication to God, and earnestly beseech Him to shed mercifully the light of His wisdom and of His counsel upon men, so that, strengthened by these heavenly gifts, they may in matters of such moment discern what is true, and may afterwards, in public and in private, at all times and with unshaken constancy, live in accordance with the truth. As a pledge of these heavenly gifts, and in witness of Our good will to you, Venerable Brothers, and to the clergy and people committed to each of you, We most lovingly grant in the Lord the Apostolic Benediction.

CHRISTIAN MARRIAGE.

Encyclical Letter, February 10, 1880.

THE hidden design of the divine wisdom, which Jesus Christ the Saviour of men came to carry out on earth, had this end in view, that, by Himself and in Himself, He should divinely renew the world, which was sinking as it were, with length of years, into decline. The Apostle Paul summed this up in words of dignity and majesty when he wrote to the Ephesians, thus: *That He might make known unto us the mystery of His will . . . . to re-establish all things in Christ that are in heaven and on earth.* *

The restoration of the supernatural order. In truth, Christ our Lord, setting Himself to fulfil the commandment which His Father had given Him, straightway imparted a new form and fresh beauty to all things, taking away the effects of their time-worn age. For He healed the wounds which the sin of our first father had inflicted on the human race; He brought all men, by nature children of wrath, into favour with God; He led to the light of truth men wearied out by long-standing errors; He renewed to every virtue those who were weakened by lawlessness of every kind; and, giving them again an inheritance of never-ending bliss, He added a sure hope that their mortal and

---
* *Ephes.* i. 9, 10.

perishable bodies should one day be partakers of immortality and of the glory of heaven. In order that these unparalleled benefits might last as long as men should be found on earth, He entrusted to His Church the continuance of His work; and, looking to future times, He commanded her to set in order whatever might have become deranged in human society, and to restore whatever might have fallen into ruin.

Many benefits conferred on the natural order itself, Although the divine renewal we have spoken of chiefly and directly affected men as constituted in the supernatural order of grace, nevertheless some of its precious and salutary fruits were also bestowed abundantly in the order of nature. Hence, not only individual men, but also the whole mass of the human race, have in every respect received no small degree of worthiness. For, so soon as Christian order was once established in the world, it became

both for individual men, happily possible for all men, one by one, to learn what God's fatherly providence is, and to dwell in it habitually, thereby fostering that hope of heavenly help which never confoundeth. From all this outflowed fortitude, self-control, constancy, and the evenness of a peaceful mind, together with many high virtues and noble deeds.

as also for Society at large, Wondrous, indeed, was the extent of dignity, steadfastness, and goodness, which thus accrued to the State as well as to the family. The authority of rulers became more just and revered; the obedience of the people more

M

ready and unforced; the union of citizens closer; the rights of dominion more secure. In very truth, the Christian religion thought of and provided for all things which are held to be advantageous in a State; so much so, indeed, that, according to St. Augustine, one cannot see how it could have offered greater help in the matter of living well and happily, had it been instituted for the single object of procuring or increasing those things which contribute to the conveniences and advantages of this mortal life.

and especially for the domestic household. Still, the purpose We have set before Us is not to recount, in detail, benefits of this kind; Our wish is rather to speak about that family union of which *Marriage* is the beginning and the foundation.

The true origin of Marriage, Venerable Brothers, is well known to all. Though the revilers of the Christian faith refuse to acknowledge the never interrupted doctrine of the Church on this subject, and have long striven to destroy the testimony of all nations and of all times, they have nevertheless failed not only to quench the powerful light of truth, but even to lessen it. We record what is to all known, and cannot be doubted by any, that God, on the sixth day of creation, having *Marriage a divine institution,* made man from the slime of the earth, and having breathed into his face the breath of life, gave him a companion, whom He miraculously took from the side of Adam when he was locked in sleep. God thus, in His most far-reaching foresight, decreed that this husband and wife should be the natural beginning of the human race, from whom it might be propagated, and preserved by an unfailing fruitfulness throughout all futurity of time. And this union of man and woman, that it might answer more fittingly to the infinitely wise counsels of God, even from that beginning manifested chiefly two most excellent properties, —deeply sealed, as it were, and signed upon it—namely, unity and perpetuity. From the Gospel we see clearly that this doctrine was declared and openly confirmed by the divine authority of Jesus Christ. He bore witness to the Jews and to His Apostles that Marriage, from its institution, should exist between two only, that is, between one man and one woman; that of two they are made, so to say, one flesh; and that the marriage-bond is by the will of God so closely and strongly made fast that no man may dissolve it or rend it asunder. *For this cause shall a man leave father and mother, and shall cleave to his wife, and they two shall be in one flesh. Therefore now they are not two, but one flesh. What, therefore, God hath joined together, let no man put asunder.* *

<small>having, from the beginning, the two properties of unity and indissolubility.</small>

<small>The primitive character of Marriage obscured by the Hebrews, through polygamy and divorce; corrupted by the Gentiles with every kind of sin.</small>

This form of marriage, however, so excellent and so pre-eminent, began to be corrupted by degrees, and to disappear among the heathen; and became even among the Jewish race clouded in a measure, and obscured. For in their midst a common custom was gradually introduced, by which it was accounted as lawful for a man to have more than one wife; and eventually when *by reason of the hardness of their*

---

* *Matt.* xxi. 5, 6.

heart,* Moses indulgently permitted them to put away their wives, the way was opened to divorce.

But the corruption and change which fell on Marriage among the Gentiles seem almost incredible, inasmuch as it was exposed in every land to floods of error and of the most shameful lusts. All nations seem, more or less, to have forgotten the true notion and origin of marriage; and thus everywhere laws were enacted with reference to Marriage, prompted to all appearance by State reasons, but not such as nature required. Solemn rites, invented at will of the lawgivers, brought about that women should, as might be, bear either the honourable name of wife or the disgraceful name of concubine; and things came to such a pitch that permission to marry, or the refusal of the permission, depended on the will of the Heads of the State, whose laws were greatly against equity or even to the highest degree unjust. Moreover, plurality of wives and husbands, the abounding source of divorces, caused the nuptial bond to be relaxed exceedingly. Hence, too, sprang up the greatest confusion as to the mutual rights and duties of husbands and wives, inasmuch as a man assumed right of dominion over his wife, ordering her to go about her business, often without any just cause; while he was himself at liberty (as St. Jerome says) "to run headlong with impunity into lust, unbridled and unrestrained, in houses of ill-fame and amongst his female slaves, as if the dignity of the persons sinned with, and not the will of the sinner, made the guilt." † When the licentiousness of a husband thus showed itself, nothing could be more piteous than the

---
* *Matt.* xix. 8.   † Hieron. Op. tom. i. col. 455.

wife, sunk so low as to be all but reckoned as a means for the gratification of passion, or for the production of offspring. Without any feeling of shame marriageable girls were bought and sold, just like so much merchandise;* and power was sometimes given to the father and to the husband to inflict capital punishment on the wife. Of necessity the offspring of such marriages as these were either reckoned among the stock in trade of the commonwealth, or held to be the property of the father of the family;† and the law permitted him to make and unmake the marriages of his children at his mere will, and even to exercise against them the monstrous power of life and death.

Jesus Christ restored marriage to its first condition. So manifold being the vices and so great the ignominies with which marriage was defiled, an alleviation and a remedy were at length bestowed from on high. Jesus Christ, Who restored our human dignity and Who perfected the Mosaic law, applied early in His ministry no little solicitude to the question of Marriage. He ennobled the marriage in Cana of Galilee by His presence, and made it memorable by the first of the miracles which He wrought:‡ and for this reason, even from that day forth, it seemed as if the beginnings of new holiness had been conferred on human marriages. Later on He brought back matrimony to the nobility of its primeval origin, by condemning the customs of the Jews in their abuse of the plurality of wives and of the power of giving bills of divorce; and still more by commanding most strictly that no one should dare to dissolve that

---
* Arnob. adv. Gent. 4.   † Dionys. Halicar. lib. ii. cc. 26, 27
‡ *John* ii.

union which God Himself had sanctioned by a bond perpetual. Hence, having set aside the difficulties which were adduced from the the law of Moses, He, in character of Supreme Lawgiver, decreed as follows concerning husbands and wives : *I say to you, that whosoever shall put away his wife, except it be for fornication, and shall marry another, committeth adultery; and he that shall marry her that is put away committeth adultery.* *

and raised it to the dignity of a Sacrament. But what was decreed and constituted in respect to Marriage by the authority of God, has been more fully and more clearly handed down to us, by tradition and the Written Word, through the Apostles, those heralds of the laws of God. To the Apostles, indeed, as our masters, are to be referred the doctrines which *our holy Fathers, the Councils, and the Tradition of the Universal Church have always taught :* † namely—that Christ our Lord raised marriage to the dignity of a Sacrament; that to husband and wife, guarded and strengthened by the heavenly grace which His merits gained for them, He gave power to attain holiness in the married state; and that, in a wondrous way, making Marriage an example of the mystical union between Himself and His Church, He not only perfected that love which is according to nature, ‡ but also made the natural union of one man with one woman far more perfect through the bond of heavenly love. Paul says to the Ephesians : *Husbands, love your wives, as Christ also loved the Church, and delivered Himself up for it, that He*

---

* *Matt.* xix. 9. † Trid. Sess. xxiv. in pr.
‡ Trid. sess. xxiv. cap. i. *de reform. matr.*

*might sanctify it. . . . . So also ought men to love their wives as their own bodies. . . . . For no man ever hated his own flesh, but nourisheth and cherisheth it, as also Christ doth the Church; because we are members of His body, of His flesh, and of His bones. For this cause shall a man leave His father and mother, and shall cleave to his wife, and they shall be two in one flesh. This is a great sacrament; but I speak in Christ and in the Church.** In like manner from the teaching of the Apostles we learn that the unity of Marriage and its perpetual indissolubility, the indispensable conditions of its very origin, must, according to the command of Christ, be holy and inviolable without exception. Paul says again : *To them that are married, not I, but the Lord commandeth that the wife depart not from her husband; and if she depart, that she remain unmarried or be reconciled to her husband.* † And again : *A woman is bound by the law as long as her husband liveth ; but if her husband die, she is at liberty.* ‡ It is for these reasons that marriage *is a great sacrament ;* § *honourable in all ;* || holy, pure, and to be reverenced as a type and symbol of most high mysteries.

<small>A higher end proposed to nuptial intercourse.</small> Furthermore, the Christian perfection and completeness of Marriage are not comprised in those points only which have been mentioned.

For, first, there has been vouchsafed to the marriage union a higher and nobler purpose than was ever previously given to it. By the command of Christ, it not only looks to the propagation of the human race, but to the bringing

---

* *Eph.* v. 25-32. † 1 *Cor.* vii. 10, 11. ‡ 1 *Cor.* vii. 39. § *Eph.* v. 32
|| *Heb.* xiii 4.

forth of children for the Church, *fellow-citizens with the saints, and the domestics of God;* * so that *a people might be born and brought up for the worship and religion of the true God and our Saviour Jesus Christ.*†

The mutual rights and duties of husbands and and wives defined.

Secondly, the mutual duties of husband and wife have been defined, and their several rights accurately established. They are bound, namely, to have such feelings for one another as to cherish always very great mutual love, to be ever faithful to their marriage-vow, and to give to one another an unfailing and unselfish help. The husband is the chief of the family, and the head of the wife. The woman, because she is flesh of his flesh, and bone of his bone, must be subject to her husband and obey him; not, indeed, as a servant, but as a companion, so that her obedience shall be wanting in neither honour nor dignity. Since the husband represents Christ, and since the wife represents the Church, let there always be, both in him who commands and in her who obeys, a heaven-born love guiding both in their respective duties. For *the husband is the head of the wife; as Christ is the head of the Church. . . . Therefore, as the Church is subject to Christ, so also let wives be to their husbands in all things.* ‡

The authority of parents over their children, and reverence of children towards their parents prescribed.

As regards children, they ought to submit to their parents and obey them, and give them honour for conscience' sake; while, on the other hand, parents are bound to give all care and watchful thought to the education of their

---
* *Eph.* ii. 19. † *Catech. Rom.* c. viii. ‡ *Eph.* v. 23, 24.

offspring and their virtuous bringing up: *Fathers, ... bring them up* (that is, your children) *in the discipline and correction of the Lord.** From this we see clearly that the duties of husbands and wives are neither few nor light ; although to married people who are good, these burdens become not only bearable but agreeable, owing to the strength which they gain through the Sacrament.

The discipline of the married state committed by Christ to the Church, which has constantly exercised this divinely conferred authority, and has provided by its laws for the due sanctity and protection of marriage.

Christ therefore, having renewed Marriage to such and so great excellence, commended and entrusted all the discipline bearing upon these matters to His Church. The Church, always and everywhere, has so used her power with reference to the marriages of Christians, that men have seen clearly how it belongs to her as of native right ; not being made hers by any human grant, but given divinely to her by the will of her Founder. Her constant and watchful care in guarding marriage, by the preservation of its sanctity, is so well understood as not to need proof. That the judgment of the Council of Jerusalem reprobated licentious and free-love,† we all know ; as also that the incestuous Corinthian was condemned by the authority of blessed Paul.‡ Again, in the very beginning of the Christian Church were repulsed and defeated, with the like unremitting determination, the efforts of many who aimed at the destruction of Christian Marriage, such as the Gnostics, Manicheans, and Montanists ; and in our own time Mormons, St. Simonians, Phalansterians, and Communists.

---

* *Eph.* vi. 4. † *Acts* xv. 29. ‡ 1 *Cor.* v. 5.

In like manner, moreover, a law of Marriage just to all, and the same for all, was enacted by the abolition of the old distinction between slaves and free-born men and women; and thus the rights of husbands and wives were made equal: for, as St. Jerome says, " with us that which is unlawful for women is unlawful for men also, and the same restraint is imposed on equal conditions." * The self-same rights also were firmly established for reciprocal affection and for the interchange of duties; the dignity of the woman was asserted and assured; and it was forbidden to the man to inflict capital punishment for adultery, or lustfully and shamelessly to violate his plighted faith.

It is also a great blessing that the Church has limited so far as is needful, the power of fathers of families, so that sons and daughters, wishing to marry, are not in any way deprived of their rightful freedom; that, for the purpose of spreading more widely the supernatural love of husbands and wives, she has decreed marriages within certain degrees of consanguinity or affinity to be null and void; that she has taken the greatest pains to safeguard Marriage, as much as is possible, from error and violence and deceit; that she has always wished to preserve the holy chasteness of the marriage bed, personal rights, the honour of husband and wife, and the security of religion.

Lastly, with such power and with such foresight of legislation has the Church guarded this divine institution, that no one who thinks rightfully of these matters can fail to see how, with regard to Marriage, she is the best guardian and defender of the human race; and how withal her wisdom has come forth victorious from the lapse of years,

---
* Oper. tom. I. col. 455.

from the assaults of men, and from the countless changes of public events.

<small>Rationalists have endeavoured to withdraw Marriage from the control of the Church, and to treat it as a mere human institution.</small>
Yet owing to the efforts of the arch-enemy of mankind, there are persons who, thanklessly casting away so many other blessings of redemption, despise also or utterly ignore the restoration of Marriage to its original perfection. It is the reproach of some of the ancients that they showed themselves the enemies of Marriage in many ways; but, in our own age, much more pernicious is the sin of those who would fain pervert utterly the nature of Marriage, perfect though it is, and complete in all its details and parts. The chief reason why they act in this way is because very many, imbued with the maxims of a false philosophy and corrupted in morals, judge nothing so unbearable as submission and obedience; and strive with all their might to bring about that not only individual men, but families also, nay indeed human society itself, may in haughty pride despise the sovereignty of God.

Now, since the family and human society at large spring from Marriage, these men will on no account allow matrimony to be subject to the jurisdiction of the Church. Nay, they endeavour to deprive it of all holiness, and so bring it within the contracted sphere of those rights which, having been instituted by man, are ruled and administered by the civil jurisprudence of the community. Wherefore it necessarily follows that they attribute all power over Marriage to civil rulers, and allow none whatever to the Church; and when the Church exercises any such power, they think that she acts either by favour of the civil authority or to its injury. Now is the time, they say, for the Heads of the State to vindicate their rights unflinchingly, and to do their best to settle all that relates to Marriage according as to them seems good.

Hence are owing *civil marriages*, commonly so called; hence laws are framed which impose impediments to Marriage; hence arise judicial sentences affecting the Marriage contract, as to whether or not it have been rightly made. Lastly, all power of prescribing and passing judgment in this class of cause is, as we see, of set purpose denied to the Catholic Church, so that no regard is paid either to her divine power or to her prudent laws. Yet under these, for so many centuries, have the nations lived on whom the light of civilisation shone bright with the wisdom of Christ Jesus.

But the right of the Church to control Marriage is seen from the sacred character inherent in it from its first institution;

Nevertheless, all they who reject what is supernatural, as well as all who profess that they worship above all things the divinity of the State, and strive to disturb whole communities with such wicked doctrines, cannot escape the charge of delusion. Marriage has God for its author, and was from the very beginning a kind of foreshadowing of the Incarnation of His Son; and therefore there abides in it a something holy and religious; not extraneous, but innate; not derived from men, but implanted by nature. Innocent III., therefore, and Honorius III., our predecessors, affirmed not falsely nor rashly that a certain sacredness of marriage rites existed ever among the faithful and unbelievers.* We call to witness the monuments of antiquity, as also the manners and customs of those peoples who, being the most civilised, had the greatest knowledge of law and equity. In the minds of all of them it was a fixed and foregone conclusion that, when Marriage was thought of, it was thought of as conjoined with religion and holiness. Hence among those, marriages were commonly celebrated with religious ceremonies, under the authority of pontiffs, and with the ministry of priests. So mighty, even in souls ignorant of heavenly doctrine, was the force of nature, of the remembrance of their origin, and of the conscience of the human race. As, then, Marriage is holy by its own power, in its own nature, and of itself, it ought not to be regulated and administered by the will of civil rulers, but by the divine authority of the Church, which alone in sacred matters professes the office of teaching.

Next, the dignity of the Sacrament must be considered; for through addition of the Sacrament the marriages of Christians have become far the noblest of all matrimonial unions. But to decree and ordain concerning the Sacrament is, by the will of Christ Himself, so much a part of the power and duty of the Church, that it is plainly absurd to maintain that even the very smallest fraction of such power has been transferred to the civil ruler.

by the dignity of a sacrament which Christ willed to apply to it;

Lastly has to be borne in mind the great weight and crucial test of history, by which it is plainly proved that the legislative and judicial authority of which We

---

* *Apud fideles et infideles existere sacramentum conjugii.* (Editor.)

are speaking has been freely and constantly used by the Church, even in times when some foolishly suppose the Head of the State either to have consented to it or connived at it. It would, for instance, be incredible and altogether absurd to assume that Christ our Lord condemned the long-standing practice of polygamy and divorce by authority delegated to Him by the procurator of the province, or the principal ruler of the Jews. And it would be equally extravagant to think that, when the Apostle Paul taught that divorces and incestuous marriages were not lawful, it was because Tiberius, Caligula, and Nero agreed with him or secretly commanded him so to teach. No man in his senses could ever be persuaded that the Church made so many laws about the holiness and indissolubility of Marriage, and the marriages of slaves with the free-born, by power received from Roman Emperors most hostile to the Christian name, whose strongest desire was to destroy by violence and murder the rising Church of Christ. Still less could any one believe this to be the case, when the law of the Church was sometimes so divergent from the civil law that Ignatius the Martyr, Justin, Athenagoras, and Tertullian publicly denounced as unjust and adulterous certain marriages which had been sanctioned by Imperial law.

by the action of our Saviour, of the Apostles, of the Pontiffs and Bishops in its regard ;

Furthermore, after all power had devolved upon the Christian Emperors, the Supreme Pontiffs and Bishops assembled in Council persisted, with the same independence and consciousness of their right, in commanding

with the united consent of Christian princes.

or forbidding in regard to Marriage whatever they judged to be profitable or expedient for the time being, however much it might seem to be at variance with the laws of the State. It is well known that, with respect to the impediments arising from the marriage bond, through vow, disparity of worship, blood relationship, certain forms of crime, and from previously plighted troth, many decrees were issued by the rulers of the Church in the Councils of Illiberis, Arles, Chalcedon, the second of Milevum, and others, which were often widely different from the decrees sanctioned by the law of the Empire. Furthermore, so far were Christian princes from arrogating any power in the matter of Christian Marriage, that they on the contrary acknowledged and declared that it belonged exclusively in all its fulness to the Church. In fact, Honorius, the younger Theodosius, and Justinian also, hesitated not to confess that the only power belonging to them in relation to Marriage was that of acting as guardians and defenders of the Holy Canons. If at any time they enacted anything by their edicts concerning impediments of marriage, they voluntarily explained the reason, affirming that they took it upon themselves so to act, by leave and authority of the Church, whose judgment they were wont to appeal to and reverently to accept, in all questions that concerned legitimacy and divorce; as also in all those points which in any way have a necessary connection with the marriage bond. The Council of Trent, therefore, had the clearest right to define that it is in the Church's power "to establish diriment impediments of matrimony," and that "matrimonial causes pertain to ecclesiastical judges."*

---

* Trid. sess. xxiv. can. 4, 12.

Let no one then be deceived by the distinction, which some Court legists have so strongly insisted upon—the distinction, namely, by virtue of which they sever the matrimonial contract from the Sacrament, with intent to hand over the contract to the power and will of the rulers of the State, while reserving questions concerning the Sacrament to the Church. A distinction, or rather severance, of this kind cannot be approved: for certain it is that in Christian Marriage the contract is inseparable from the Sacrament; and that, for this reason, the contract cannot be true and legitimate without being a Sacrament as well. For Christ our Lord added to Marriage the dignity of a Sacrament; but Marriage is the contract itself, whenever that contract is lawfully concluded.

In Christian Marriage the contract inseparable from the sacrament.

Marriage, moreover, is a Sacrament, because it is a holy sign which gives grace, showing forth an image of the mystical nuptials of Christ with the Church. But the form and image of these nuptials is shown precisely by the very bond of that most close union in which man and woman are bound together in one; which bond is nothing else but the marriage itself. Hence it is clear that among Christians every true marriage is, in itself and by itself, a Sacrament; and that nothing can be farther from the truth than to say that the Sacrament is a certain added ornament, or outward endowment, which can be separated and torn away from the contract at the caprice of man. Neither therefore by reasoning can it be shown, nor by any testimony of history be proved, that power over the marriages of Christians has ever lawfully been handed over to the rulers of the State. If, in this matter, the right of any one else has ever been violated, no one can truly say that it has been violated by the Church.

The evils arising from desecrated marriages considered. Would that the teaching of those who reject what is supernatural, besides being full of falsehood and injustice, were not also the fertile source of much detriment and calamity! But it is easy to see at a glance the greatness of the evil which unhallowed marriages have brought, and ever will bring, on the whole of human society.

From the beginning of the world, indeed, it was divinely ordained that things instituted by God and by Nature should be proved by us to be the more profitable and salutary the more they remain unchanged in their full integrity. For God, the Maker of all things, well knowing what was good for the institution and preservation of each of His creatures, so ordered them by His will and mind that each might adequately attain the end for which it was made. If the rashness or the wickedness of human agency venture to change or disturb that order of things which has been constituted with fullest foresight, then the designs of infinite wisdom and usefulness begin either to be hurtful or cease to be profitable, partly because through the change undergone they have lost their power of benefiting, and partly because God chooses to inflict punishment on the pride and audacity of man. Now those who deny that marriage is holy, and who relegate it, stripped of all holiness, among the class of common things, uproot thereby the foundations of nature, not only resisting the designs of Providence, but, so far as they can, destroying

N

the order that God has ordained. No one, therefore, should wonder if from such insane and impious attempts there spring up a crop of evils pernicious in the highest degree both to the salvation of souls and to the safety of the commonwealth.

If, then, we consider the end of the divine institution of marriage, we shall see very clearly that God intended it to be a most fruitful source of individual benefit and of public welfare. Not only, in strict truth, was marriage instituted for the propagation of the human race, but also that the lives of husbands and wives might be made better and happier. This comes about in many ways: by their lightening each others' burdens through mutual help; by constant and faithful love; by having all their possessions in common; and by the heavenly grace which flows from the Sacrament. Marriage also can do much for the good of families: for, so long as it is conformable to nature and in accordance with the counsels of God, it has power to strengthen union of heart in the parents; to secure the holy education of children; to attemper the authority of the father by the example of the divine authority; to render children obedient to their parents, and servants obedient to their masters. From such marriages as these the State may rightly expect a race of citizens animated by a good spirit and filled with reverence and love for God, recognising it their duty to obey those who rule justly and lawfully, to love all, and to injure no one.

These many and glorious fruits were ever the product of Marriage, so long as it retained those gifts of holiness, unity and indissolubility, from which proceeded all its fertile and saving power; nor can any one doubt but that it would always have brought forth such fruits, at all times, and in all places, had it been under the power and guardianship of the Church, the trustworthy preserver and protector of these gifts. But now there is a spreading wish to supplant natural and divine law by human law; and hence has begun a gradual extinction of that most excellent ideal of marriage which Nature herself had impressed on the soul of man, and sealed, as it were, with her own seal; nay, more, even in Christian Marriages this power, productive of so great good, has been weakened by the sinfulness of man. Of what advantage is it, if a State can institute nuptials estranged from the Christian religion, which is the mother of all good cherishing all sublime virtues, quickening and urging us to everything that is the glory of a lofty and generous soul? When the Christian religion is rejected and repudiated, marriage sinks of necessity into the slavery of man's vicious nature and vile passions, and finds but little protection in the help of natural goodness. A very torrent of evil has flowed from this source, not only into private families, but also into States. For the salutary fear of God being removed, and there being no longer that refreshment in toil which is nowhere more abounding than in the Christian religion, it very often happens, as from facts is evident, that the mutual services and duties of marriage seem almost unbearable; and thus very many yearn for the loosening of the tie which they believe to be woven by human law and of their own will, whenever incompatibility of temper, or quarrels, or the violation of the marriage vow, or mutual consent, or other reasons induce them to think that it would be well to be set free. Then, if they are hindered by law from carrying out this shameless desire, they contend that the laws are iniquitous, inhuman, and at variance with the rights of free citizens; adding that every effort should be made to repeal such enactments, and to introduce a more humane code sanctioning divorce.

These have led to the law of divorce, Now, however much the legislators of these our days may wish to guard themselves against the impiety of men such as we have been speaking of, they are unable to do so, seeing that they profess to hold and defend the very same principles of jurisprudence; and hence they have to go with the times, and render divorce easily obtainable. History itself shows this; for, to pass over other instances, we find that, at the close of the last century, divorces were sanctioned by law in that upheaval, or rather, as it might be called, conflagration in France, when society was wholly degraded by the abandoning of God. Many at the present time would fain have those laws re-enacted, because they wish God and His Church to be altogether exiled and excluded from the midst of human society, madly thinking that in such laws a final remedy must be sought for that moral corruption which is advancing with rapid strides.

the fruitful parent of fresh evils, Truly, it is hardly possible to describe how great are the evils that flow from divorce. Matrimonial contracts are by it made variable; mutual kindness is weakened; deplorable inducements to unfaithfulness are supplied; harm is done to the education and training of children; occasion is afforded for the breaking up of homes; the seeds of dissension are sown among families;

the dignity of womanhood is lessened and brought low, and women run the risk of being deserted after having ministered to the pleasures of men. Since, then, nothing has such power to lay waste families and destroy the mainstay of kingdoms as the corruption of morals, it is easily seen that divorces are in the highest degree hostile to the prosperity of families and States, springing as they do from the depraved morals of the people, and, as experience shows us, opening out a way to every kind of evil-doing in public alike and in private life.

as experience invariably testifies. Further still, if the matter be duly pondered, we shall clearly see these evils to be the more especially dangerous, because, divorce once being tolerated, there will be no restraint powerful enough to keep it within the bounds marked out or presurmised. Great indeed is the force of example, and even greater still the might of passion. With such incitements it must needs follow that the eagerness for divorce, daily spreading by devious ways, will seize upon the minds of many like a virulent contagious disease, or like a flood of water bursting through every barrier. These are truths that doubtlessly are all clear in themselves; but they will become clearer yet, if we call to mind the teachings of experience. So soon as the road to divorce began to be made smooth by law, at once quarrels, jealousies, and judicial separations, largely increased; and such shamelessness of life followed, that men who had been in favour of these divorces repented of what they had done, and feared that, if they did not carefully seek a remedy by repealing the law, the State itself might come to ruin.

The Romans of old are said to have shrunk with horror from the first examples of divorce: but ere long all sense of decency was blunted in their soul; the meagre restraint of passion died out, and the marriage vow was so often broken, that what some writers have affirmed would seem to be true—namely, women used to reckon years not by the change of Consuls, but of their husbands.

In like manner, at the beginning, Protestants allowed legalized divorces in certain although but few cases, and yet, from the affinity of circumstances of like kind, the number of divorces increased to such extent in Germany, America and elsewhere, that all wise thinkers deplored the boundless corruption of morals, and judged the recklessness of the laws to be simply intolerable.

Even in Catholic States the like evil existed. For whenever at any time divorce was introduced, the abundance of misery that followed far exceeded all that the framers of the law could have foreseen. In fact, many lent their minds to contrive all kinds of fraud and device, and by accusations of cruelty, violence and adultery, to feign grounds for the dissolution of the matrimonial bond of which they had grown weary; and all this with so great havoc to morals that an amendment of the laws was deemed to be urgently needed.

Can any one, therefore, doubt that laws in favour of divorce would have a result equally baneful and calamitous were they to be passed in these our days? There exists not, indeed, in the projects and enactments of men any power to change the character and tendency which things have received from nature. Those men therefore show but little wisdom in the idea they have formed of the well-being of the commonwealth, who think that the inherent character of marriage can be perverted with impunity; and who, disregarding the sanctity of religion and of the Sacrament, seem to wish to degrade and dishonour marriage more basely than was done even by heathen laws. Indeed, if they do not change their views, not only private families, but all public society will have unceasing cause to fear lest they should be miserably driven into that general confusion and overthrow of order which is even now the wicked aim of Socialists and Communists.

Thus, we most clearly see how foolish and senseless it is to expect any public good from divorce, when, on the contrary, it• tends to the certain destruction of society.

The Church, by reason of her care to protect the sanctity and perpetuity of the married state, deserves well of all nations.

It must consequently be acknowledged that the Church has deserved exceedingly well of all nations by her ever-watchful care in guarding the sanctity and the indissolubility of Marriage. Again, no small amount of gratitude is owing to her for having, during the last hundred years, openly denounced the wicked laws which have grievously offended on this particular subject; as well as for her having branded with anathema the baneful heresy obtaining among Protestants touching divorce and separation; also for having in many ways condemned the habitual dissolution of marriage among the Greeks; for having declared invalid all marriages contracted upon the understanding that they may be at some future time dissolved; and lastly, for having, from the earliest times, repudiated the imperial laws which disastrously favoured divorce.

As often, indeed, as the Supreme Pontiffs have resisted the most powerful amongst rulers, in their threatening demands that divorces carried out by them should be confirmed by the Church, so often must we account them to have been contending for the safety, not only of religion, but also of the human race. For this reason all generations of men will admire the proofs of unbending courage which are to be found in the decrees of Nicholas I. against Lothair; of Urban II. and Paschal II. against Philip I. of France; of Celestine III. and Innocent III. against Alphonsus of Leon and Philip II. of France; of Clement VII. and Paul III. against Henry VIII.; and lastly, of Pius VII., that holy and courageous Pontiff, against Napoleon I., when at the height of his prosperity and in the fulness of his power.

This being so, all rulers and administrators of the State who are desirous of following the dictates of reason and wisdom, and anxious for the good of their people, ought to make up their minds to keep the holy laws of marriage intact; and to make use of the proffered aid of the Church for securing the safety of morals and the happiness of families, rather than suspect her of hostile intention, and falsely and wickedly accuse her of violating the civil law.

The Church instead of opposing does greatly aid the Civil power.

They should do this the more readily because the Catholic Church, though powerless in any way to abandon the duties of her office or the defence of her authority, still very greatly inclines to kindness and indulgence whenever they are consistent with the safety of her rights and the sanctity of her duties. Wherefore she makes no decrees in relation to marriage without having regard to the state of the body politic and the condition of the general public; and has besides more than once mitigated, as far as possible, the enactments of her own laws, when there were just and weighty reasons. Moreover she is not unaware, and never calls in doubt, that the Sacrament of Marriage, being instituted for the preservation and increase of the human race, has a necessary relation to circumstances of life, which, though connected with marriage, belong to the civil order, and about which the State rightly makes strict enquiry and justly promulgates decrees.

Concord between both these parties is to be greatly desired. Yet no one doubts that Jesus Christ, the Founder of the Church, willed her sacred power to be distinct from the Civil power, and each power to be free and unshackled in its own sphere: with this condition, however, —a condition good for both, and of advantage to all men—that union and concord should be maintained between them; and that on those questions which are, though in different ways, of common right and authority, the power to which secular matters have been entrusted should happily and becomingly depend on the other power which has in its charge the interests of heaven. In such arrangement and harmony is found not only the best line of action for each power, but also the most opportune and efficacious method of helping men in all that pertains to their life here, and to their hope of salvation hereafter. For, as We have shown in former Encyclical Letters, the intellect of man is greatly ennobled by the Christian faith, and made better able to shun and banish all error, while faith borrows in turn no little help from the intellect; and in like manner, when the Civil power is on friendly terms with the sacred authority of the Church, there accrues to both a great increase of usefulness. The dignity of the one is exalted, and so long as religion is its guide it will never rule unjustly; while the other receives help of protection and defence for the public good of the faithful.

The Pope offers his co-operation to temporal rulers.

Being moved, therefore, by these considerations, as We have exhorted rulers at other times, so still more earnestly We exhort them now, to concord and friendly feeling; and We are the first to stretch out Our hand to them with fatherly benevolence, and to offer to them the help of Our supreme authority,—a help which is the more necessary at this time when, in public opinion, the authority of rulers is wounded and enfeebled. Now that the minds of so many are inflamed with a reckless spirit of liberty, and men are wickedly endeavouring to get rid of every restraint of authority, however legitimate it may be, the public safety demands that both powers should unite their strength to avert the evils which are hanging, not only over the Church, but also over Civil society.

He strongly exhorts all bishops to urge on the faithful that they ever bear in mind

But, while earnestly exhorting all to a friendly union of will, and beseeching God, the Prince of Peace, to infuse a love of concord into all hearts, We cannot, Venerable Brothers, refrain from urging you more and more to fresh earnestness, and zeal, and watchfulness, though we know that these are already very great. With every effort and with all authority, strive, as much as you are able, to preserve whole and undefiled among the people committed to your charge the doctrine which Christ our Lord taught us; which the Aposles, the interpreters of the will of God, have handed down; and which the Catholic Church has herself scrupulously guarded, and commanded to be believed in all ages by the faithful of Christ.

The Divine origin of marriage, its supernatural dignity, unity and perpetuity. Let special care be taken that the people be well instructed in the precepts of Christian wisdom, so that they may always remember that Marriage was not instituted by the will of man, but, from the very beginning, by the authority and command of God; that it does not admit of plurality of wives or husbands; that Christ, the author of the New Covenant, raised it from a rite of nature to be a Sacrament, and gave to His Church legislative and judicial power with regard to the bond of union. On this point the very greatest care must be taken to instruct them, lest their minds should be led into error by the unsound conclusions of adversaries who desire that the Church should be deprived of that power.

In like manner all ought to understand clearly that, if there be any union of a man and woman among the faithful of Christ which is not a Sacrament, such union has not the force and nature of a proper marriage; that although contracted in accordance with the laws of the State, it cannot be more than a rite or custom introduced by the Civil law. Further, the Civil law can deal with and decide those matters alone which in the Civil order spring from Marriage, and which cannot possibly exist, as is evident, unless there be a true and lawful cause for them, that is to say, the nuptial bond. It is of the greatest consequence to husband and wife that all these things should be known and well understood by them, in order that they may conform to the laws of the State, if there be no objection on the part of the Church; for the Church wishes the effects of Marriage to be guarded in all possible ways, and that no harm may come to the children.

In the great confusion of opinions, however, which day by day is spreading more and more widely, it should further be known that no power can dissolve the bond of Christian Marriage whenever this has been ratified and consummated; and that, of a consequence, those husbands and wives are guilty of a manifest crime who plan, for whatsoever reason, to be united in a second marriage before the first one has been ended by death. When, indeed, matters have come to such a pitch that it seems impossible for them to live together any longer, then the Church allows them to live apart, and strives at the same time to soften the evils of this separation by such remedies and helps as are suited to their condition; yet she never ceases to endeavour to bring about a reconciliation, and never despairs of doing so. But these are extreme cases; and they would seldom exist if men and women entered into the married state with proper dispositions, not influenced by passion, but entertaining right ideas of the duties of Marriage and of its noble purpose; neither would they anticipate their marriage by a series of sins drawing down upon them the wrath of God.

To sum up all in a few words: there would be a calm and quiet constancy in Marriage, if married people would gather strength and life from the virtue of religion alone, which imparts to us resolution and fortitude; for religion would enable them to bear tranquilly and even gladly the trials of their state: such as, for instance, the faults that they discover in one another, the difference of temper and character, the weight of a mother's cares, the wearing anxiety about the education of children, reverses of fortune, and the sorrows of life.

Mixed marriages to be avoided. Care also must be taken that they do not easily enter into Marriage with those who are not Catholics; for when minds do not agree as to the observances of religion, it is scarcely possible to hope for agreement in other things. Other reasons also proving that persons should turn with dread from such marriages are chiefly these: that they give occasion to forbidden association and communion in religious matters; endanger the faith of the Catholic partner; are a hindrance to the proper education of the children; and often lead to a mixing up truth and falsehood, and to the belief that all religions are equally good.

Lastly, since We well know that none should be excluded from Our charity, We commend, Venerable Brothers, to your fidelity and piety those unhappy persons who, carried away by the heat of passion, and being utterly indifferent to their salvation, live wickedly together without the bond of lawful marriage. Let your utmost care be exercised in bringing such persons back to their duty; and, both by your own efforts and by those of good men who will consent to help you, strive by every means that they may see how wrongly they have acted; that they may do penance; and that they may be induced to enter into a lawful marriage according to the Catholic rite.

You will at once see, Venerable Brothers, that the doctrine and precepts in relation to Christian Marriage, which We have thought good to communicate to you in this Letter, tend no less to the preservation of civil society than to the everlasting salvation of souls. May God grant that, by reason of their gravity and importance, minds may everywhere be found docile and ready to obey them! For this end let us all suppliantly, with humble prayer, implore the help of the Blessed and Immaculate Virgin Mary, that our hearts being quickened to the obedience of faith, she may show herself our mother and our helper. With equal earnestness let us ask the Princes of the Apostles, Peter and Paul, the destroyers of heresies, the sowers of the seed of truth, to save the human race by their powerful patronage from the deluge of errors that is surging afresh.

In the meantime, as an earnest of heavenly gifts, and a testimony of Our special benevolence, We grant you all, Venerable Brothers, and to the people confided to your charge, from the depths of Our heart, the Apostolic Benediction.

THE RIGHT ORDERING OF CHRISTIAN LIFE.

Encyclical Letter, December 30, 1888.

AT the close of the year in which, by the singular blessing and benefit of God, We have in sound health celebrated the fiftieth anniversary of Our priesthood, We naturally look back upon the past months, and with great pleasure recall to memory each and all of them. And not without reason: for while the event, so far as it regarded Us personally, was of itself neither great nor wonderful, it has moved the hearts of men in an unusual manner, and has been celebrated with so many manifestations of joy and congratulation, that nothing was left to be desired. This general joy was indeed most pleasing to Us, and most gratifying; but what We valued most in connection with it was the significance of these heartfelt demonstrations, and the constancy of faith which they so unmistakably displayed. For the congratulations which came to Us from all sides expressed clearly this fact, that in all places the minds and hearts of men are turned to the Vicar of Jesus Christ; that, in the many evils which press upon us from every quarter, men look with confidence to the Apostolic See as to an ever-flowing and ever pure source of salvation; and that, in every land where the Catholic religion flourishes, the Roman Church, mother, and mistress of all Churches, is reverenced and honoured, as is right and fitting, with one mind and with ardent love.

For these reasons We have often during the past months lifted up Our eyes to the ever holy and eternal God, in thanksgiving for the most gracious gift of life bestowed upon Us, and for the many consolations vouchsafed to Us in Our sorrows; and during all this time We have used every occasion of showing Our gratitude to those to whom it was due. Now, however, the closing days of the year and of the Jubilee bid Us renew the recollection of benefits received; and, to Our very great satisfaction, the whole Church is joining with us in fresh thanksgiving. At the same time We anxiously wish by this Letter to declare publicly that as so many testimonies of devotion and kindness and love have done much to lighten Our burden, so too a grateful remembrance of them will live always in Our mind.

The Jubilee an occasion of great spiritual benefit to the world. But a holier and higher duty yet remains. For, in this affectionate and extraordinary eagerness to shew honour to the Roman Pontiff, We seem called upon to acknowledge the power and the design of God, Who often draws, and alone can draw, the beginnings of great good from events of the smallest moment. For God, in His most loving providence, seems to have wished to arouse faith in the midst of widespread disbelief, and to recall the Christian people to the pursuit of a higher life. Wherefore We must strive diligently that, laying the foundation of good, a favourable change may be inaugurated, and that the intentions of God may be both understood and put in practice. The obedience shown to the Apostolic See will indeed be full and perfect, if, joined with the admiration for Christian virtue, it lead to the salvation of souls—the only end worth seeking, and one which will abide for ever.

Christian Life. In the exercise of the high Apostolic office bestowed upon Us by the goodness of God, We have many times, as in duty bound, undertaken the defence of truth, and have striven to expound particularly that teaching which seemed the most opportune for the public welfare, so that, in seeking the truth, all might watchfully and carefully avoid the dangers of error. But now, as a loving parent of his children, We wish to address all Christians, and in simple homely words to exhort all and each to lead a holy life. For, beyond the mere profession of faith, Christian virtues and practices are necessary for the Christian; and upon these depend, not only the eternal salvation of souls, but also the stable peace and true prosperity of the human family and of society.

The reign of the threefold lust. If we inquire into the kind of life men everywhere lead, it is impossible for any one to avoid the conclusion that public and private morals differ vastly from the precepts of the Gospel. Too sadly, alas! do the words of the Apostle St. John apply to our age: *All that is in the world, is the concupiscence of the flesh, and the concupiscence of the eyes, and the pride of life.* * For in truth most men, with little heed as to whence they have come or to whither they are going, place all their thoughts and all

---
* 1 *John* ii. 16.

their care upon the vain and fleeting goods of this life; and, contrary to nature and right order, they voluntarily give themselves up to serve things of which their reason tells them they should be the masters. It is a short step from the desire of comfort and luxury to the striving after the means to obtain them. Hence arises the unbridled eagerness to become rich which binds those whom it possesses, and while they are seeking the gratification of their passion, hurries them along, often without reference to justice or injustice, and not unfrequently even with insolent contempt for the penury of others. Thus, very many who live in luxury call themselves the brethren of the multitudes whom in the depths of their hearts they despise. With minds puffed up with pride, they strive to be subject to no law, and to have respect for no authority.

Its sources.

They call self-love liberty, and think themselves *born free like a wild ass's colt.** Snares and temptations to sin abound; impious and immoral dramas are exhibited on the stage; books and the daily press jeer at virtue and ennoble crime; and the fine arts themselves, which were intended for virtuous use and for rightful recreation, are made to minister to depraved passions. Nor can we look to the future without fear; for new seeds of evil are continually being sown broadcast in the hearts of the rising generation. As for the public schools, it is well known to you that there is no ecclesiastical authority left in them; and during the years when tender minds should be trained carefully and

Bad books and licentious plays.

Godless education.

---

* *Job* xi. 12.

conscientiously in Christian virtue, the precepts of religion are for the most part even left untaught. Youths somewhat advanced in age encounter a still graver peril, namely, from evil teaching; which is of such a kind as to deceive them by misleading words, instead of filling them with a knowledge of what is true. For many now-a-days seek to learn truth by the aid of reason alone, putting divine faith entirely aside; and, through the exclusion of this strength and of this light, they fall into many errors and fail to discover the truth. They teach, for instance, that matter alone exists in the world; that men and beasts have the same origin and a like nature; and some even there are who go so far as to doubt the existence of God, the Ruler and Maker of the World, or to err most grievously, like unto the heathen, as to His Divine Nature. Hence the very essence and form of virtue, of justice and of duty, are of necessity distorted. Thus it is that, while they hold up to admiration the high authority of reason, and unduly extol the subtlety of the human intellect, they fall into the just punishment of pride through ignorance of what is of the greatest importance. When the mind has thus been poisoned, the moral character becomes at the same time deeply and substantially corrupt; and so diseased a state can be cured only with the utmost difficulty in this class of men, because on the one side their opinions vitiate the judgment of what is right, and on the other they have not the light of Christian faith, which is the principle and foundation of all righteousness.

The offspring of Godlessness.
Daily we see, with our own eyes, as it were, the numerous evils that afflict all classes of men from these causes. Poisonous doctrines have corrupted both public and private

life; rationalism, materialism, and atheism, have begotten socialism, communism, and nihilism—fatal and pestilential evils, which naturally, and almost necessarily, flow forth from such principles. In good sooth, if the Catholic religion may be rejected with impunity, whose divine origin is made clear by such unmistakable signs, why should not all other forms of religion be rejected, when it is clear that they have not the same evidence of truth? If the soul is by nature one with the body, and if therefore no hope of a happy eternity remains when the body dies, what reason is there why man should endure toil and suffering here in the endeavour to subject the appetites to right reason? The highest good of man will consist in enjoying the comforts and pleasures of life, and since there is absolutely no one who does not by an instinct and impulse of nature strive after happiness, every man will naturally lay hands on all he can, in the hope of living happily on the spoils of others. Nor will there be any power mighty enough to bridle passions when fully set astir; for, if the supreme and eternal law, which commands what is right and forbids what is wrong, be rejected, it follows that the power of law is thwarted, and that all authority is loosened. Hence the bonds of civil society will be utterly shattered, when every man is driven by insatiable greed to a perpetual struggle, some striving to keep what they possess, others to obtain what they covet. Such is more or less the spirit and tone of our age.

The remedy, being beyond human resource

There is, nevertheless, some consolation for us, even while looking at existing evils, and we may lift up our heart in good hope. For God *created all things that they might be: and He made the nations of the earth for health.** But as all this world cannot be upheld save by the will and providence of Him Who called it out of nothing, so also can men be healed only by the power of Him by Whose goodness they were recalled from death to life. For Jesus Christ redeemed the human race once by the abundant shedding of His blood; and the efficacy of this great work and gift is for all ages: *Neither is there salvation in any other.*† Hence they who strive by the enforcement of law to extinguish the ever-growing flame of popular passions, strive indeed for what is right and just; but they will labour with little or no result, so long as they obstinately reject the power of the Gospel and refuse the assistance of the Church. These evils can be cured only by a change of principles, and by returning in public and private conduct to Jesus Christ and to a Christian rule of life.

Must come from Jesus Christ.

Now the whole essence of a Christian life is not to take part in the corruption of the world, but to oppose constantly any indulgence in that corruption. This is taught by all the words and actions, by all the laws and institutions, by the very life and death of Jesus Christ, *the author and finisher of faith.* ‡ Hence, however strongly we are drawn back by our evil nature and the profligacy that is around us, it is our duty to run to the *fight proposed to us*,§ armed and prepared with the same courage and the same weapons as He Who, *having joy set before Him, endured the cross.* ‖ Wherefore men are bound to consider and understand this above all, that it is contrary to the

---
* *Wisd.* i. 14.   † *Acts* iv. 12.   ‡ *Heb.* xii. 2.   § *Heb.* xii. 1.
‖ *Heb.* xii. 2.

profession and duty of a Christian to follow, as they are wont to do, every kind of pleasure, to shrink from the hardship attending a virtuous life, and to allow oneself all that gratifies and delights the senses. *They that are Christ's have crucified their flesh, with the vices and concupiscences.* * Hence it follows that they who are not accustomed to suffer, and to disregard ease and pleasure, belong not to Christ. By the infinite goodness of God, man was restored to the hope of an immortal life from which he had been cut off; but he cannot attain to it if he strives not to walk in the very footsteps of Christ, and to conform his mind and life to that of Christ by meditating on His example. Therefore this is not a counsel, but a duty; and the duty, not only of those who desire a more perfect life, but of all,—*always bearing about in our body the mortification of Jesus.* † How else shall the natural law, which commands man to live virtuously, be kept? For by holy baptism the sin which we contracted at birth is taken away; but the evil and perverse roots which sin has planted in our hearts are by no means removed. That part of man which is without reason, although harmless to those who fight manfully by the grace of Christ, nevertheless struggles with reason for supremacy, disturbs the whole soul, and tyrannically bends the will away from virtue with such power that we cannot escape vice or do our duty except by a daily struggle. The Council of Trent says: "This holy synod teaches that in the baptised there remains concupiscence or an inclination

[Marginal note: A Christian is bound not to seek after pleasure and fly from labour.]

---

* *Gal.* v. 24.   † 2 *Cor.* iv. 10.

to evil, which, being left to be fought against, cannot hurt those who, instead of yielding to it, manfully fight against it by the grace of Jesus Christ; *for he who hath lawfully striven shall be crowned.** There is in this struggle a degree of valour to which only a very perfect virtue attains, such as belongs to those who, by putting to flight impulses opposed to right reason, have made such advances in virtue as to seem almost to live a heavenly life on earth. Granted that few attain excellence so great; yet, even the philosophy of the ancients taught that every man should conquer his evil desires; and still more and with greater care should those do so who, from daily contact with the world, are more sorely tempted—unless it be foolishly thought that where the danger is greater watchfulness is less needed, or that they whose maladies are most grievous need medicine more seldom.

The struggle with our passions brings even temporal blessings. But the toil which has to be borne in this conflict is compensated by great blessings, over and above its eternal reward in heaven; and particularly because by the quelling of the passions, nature is in a measure restored to its original dignity. For man has been born under a law that the soul should rule the body, and that the appetites should be restrained by mind and reason; and hence it follows that to restrain evil passions striving for the mastery over us is our noblest and greatest freedom. Moreover, it is difficult to see what can be expected of a man, even as a member of society, who is not thus disposed. Will any one be inclined to do right who has been accustomed to make self-love the sole rule of

---

* Sess. v. can. 5.

what he should do or avoid doing? No man can be high-souled, or kind, or merciful, or restrained, who has not learnt to conquer self, and to despise all worldly things when opposed to virtue.

The duty of mortification. Nor must We refrain from affirming that it seems to have been determined in the designs of God that there should be no salvation for men without struggle and pain. Indeed, when God gave to man pardon for sin, He gave it under the condition that His only-begotten Son should pay its just and due penalty; and though Jesus Christ might have satisfied divine justice in other ways, nevertheless He preferred to satisfy it by the utmost suffering and the sacrifice of His life. Therefore He has imposed it upon His followers as a law signed with His blood, that their life should be an endless strife with the vices of their age. What made the Apostles unconquerable in their mission of teaching truth to the world? What strengthened our countless martyrs in bearing witness by their blood to the Christian faith? Their more than readiness to obey fearlessly this law. All who have taken heed to live a Christian life and to seek after virtue have trodden the same path. We too must walk along this road, if we desire to assure either our own salvation or that of others. Therefore, in the unbounded licence that prevails, it is necessary for everyone to guard manfully against the allurements of luxury; and since on every side there is so much pretentious display of enjoyment in wealth, the soul must be strengthened against the dangerous snare of wealth, lest, in striving after what are called the good things of life, which cannot satisfy and soon fade away, the soul should lose *the treasure in heaven which faileth not.* Finally, it is a further matter of deep grief that free-thought and evil example have had such an influence in enfeebling the minds of men, as to make many ashamed of the name of Christian—a shame which is the sign either of abandoned wickedness or of extreme cowardice. Each of these is detestable, and each injurious in the extreme. For what salvation remains for men, or on what hope can they rely, if they cease to glory in the name of Jesus Christ, if they openly and constantly refuse to live by the precepts of the gospel? It is a common complaint that the age is barren of courageous men. Bring back into vogue a Christian rule of life, and the minds of men will forthwith regain their strength and constancy.

Prayer.

But man's power of itself is not equal to the responsibility of so many and such various duties. As we must ask of God our daily bread for the sustenance of the body, so must we pray to Him for strength of soul that we may be sustained in virtue. Hence that universal condition and law of our life, which We have said is a perpetual warfare, brings with it the necessity of prayer to God. For, as is well and gracefully said by St. Augustine, devout prayer passes beyond the world's space, and calls down the mercy of God from heaven. In order to conquer the assaults of our passions' and the snares of the devil, lest we be led into evil, we are commanded to seek the divine help in the words, *Pray that ye enter not into temptation.* * How much more is this necessary, if we wish to labour profitably for the salvation of others also? Christ our Lord, the only-begotten

---

* *Matt.* xxvi. 41.

Son of God, the source of all grace and virtue, first showed by example what He taught in word : *He passed the whole night in the prayer of God ;* * and when nigh to the sacrifice of His life, *He prayed the longer.*† The frailty of nature would be much less perilous, and the moral character less weak and languid, if that divine precept of prayer were not so much disregarded and treated almost with dislike. God is easily appeased. He desires to do good to men, having clearly promised to give His grace in abundance to those who ask for it. Nay, He even invites men to ask, and almost insists upon their asking, with most loving words : *I say unto you, ask, and it shall be given to you: seek and you shall find: knock and it shall be opened unto you.* ‡ And that we may have no fear in doing this with all confidence and familiarity, He makes use of tender phrases, comparing Himself to a most loving father who desires nothing so much as the love of his children : *If you then, being evil, know how to give good gifts to your children: how much more will your Father, Who is in heaven, give good things to them that ask Him ?* §

Its fruits. Whoever considers these things will not wonder at the efficacy of human prayer seeming so great to St. John Chrysostom that he thought it might be compared with the divine power. For, as God created all things by His word, so man by prayer obtains whatever he wills. Nothing has so great a power to obtain grace for us as prayer when rightly made ; for it contains the motives by which God easily allows Himself to be appeased and to incline to

---
* *Luke* vi. 12.   † *Luke* xxii. 43.   ‡ *Luke* xi. 9.   § *Matt.* vii. 11.

mercy. In prayer we separate ourselves from things of earth; filled with the thought of God alone, we become conscious of our human weakness; and therefore, resting in the goodness and embrace of our Heavenly Father, we seek refuge in the power of Him Who created us. We approach the Author of all good as if pressing Him to look upon our weak souls, unsteadfast strength, and great poverty; and, full of hope, we implore His aid and guardianship, Who alone can heal our infirmities, and give help to us in our weakness and misery. By such a condition of mind, in which, as is fitting, we think humbly of ourselves, God is greatly moved to mercy, for *God resisteth the proud, but to the humble He giveth grace.* *

Let, then, the habit of prayer be sacred to all; let the mind and heart and voice pray together; and let our life be in conformity with our prayer, so that, by keeping the divine laws, the course of our days may seem a continual ascent towards God.

Faith now restored and increased by prayer. The virtue of prayer of which we are speaking is, like other virtues, produced and nourished by divine faith. For God is the Author of all true and alone desirable blessings; and to Him also we owe our knowledge of His infinite goodness, and of the merits of Jesus our Redeemer. But, on the other hand, nothing is more fitted for the nourishment and increase of faith than the pious habit of prayer. And the need of the virtue of faith is seen plainly at this our time through its weakness in most men, and its absence in so many. For faith is especially the source whereby not only each one's life

* 1 *Peter* v. 5.

may be amended, but also right judgment may be obtained as to those matters which by their conflict hinder States from living in peace and security. If the multitude thirsts and raves for excessive liberty; if the indignation of the lower orders is with difficulty constrained; if the greed of the wealthier classes is insatiable, and if to these be added other evils of the same kind which We have elsewhere fully set forth, it will be found that nothing can remedy them more fully or more surely than Christian faith.

The example of the Clergy. And here it is fitting that We should turn Our thoughts and words to you whom God has made His helpers, by giving you His divine power to dispense His mysteries. If the sources of public and private moral welfare are examined, it will, without doubt, be found that the lives of the clergy may be of immense influence. Let them therefore remember that they have been called by Jesus Christ *the light of the world;* and that "the soul of the priest should shine like a light illuminating the whole world."* The light of learning, and this in no small degree, is needed in the priest, because it is his duty to fill others with wisdom, to overcome error, and to be a guide to the many in the steep and slippery paths of life. Learning, however, must above all be accompanied by innocence of life, because in the reformation of man example avails far more than precept. *Let your light shine before men, that they may see your good works.*† The meaning of this divine precept is, that the perfection of virtue in priests should be such that they should be like a mirror to the rest of men. "Nothing leads others

---
* S. John Chrysost *De Sac.* l. 3, c. 1.   † *Matt.* v. 16.

more surely to the love and worship of God than the life and example of those dedicated to the divine ministry: for, since they are separated from the world and placed in a higher sphere, others look on them as on a mirror, to seek from them an example which they may follow."* Therefore, if all men must watchfully take heed against the allurements of sin, and against a too eager seeking after fleeting pleasures, it is clear that priests ought to do the same much more faithfully and steadfastly. But it is not enough for them merely to restrain their passions: their sacred dignity requires of them in addition the habit of stringent self-denial, and that they should devote all the powers of their soul, particularly the intellect and will, which hold the highest powers in man, to the service of Christ. "If thou hast a mind to leave all," says St. Bernard, "remember to reckon thyself among the things that thou wishest to abandon—nay, deny thyself first and before everything." † Not until their soul is unshackled and free from every unhallowed desire, will priests have a ready and generous zeal for the salvation of others, and without this they cannot properly secure their own. "One thing only shall they seek and rejoice at in those subject to them, in one thing only shall they glory—to make of them, if possible, a perfect people. For this they will strive in every way, with great labour of mind and body, in toil and suffering, in hunger and thirst, in cold and nakedness."‡ Frequent meditation upon the things of heaven wonderfully nourishes and strengthens virtue of this kind, and makes it always ready and fearless of the greatest

---

* Con. Trid. Sess. xxii. 1, de Ref. † *Declam.*, c. 1.
‡ S. Bern., *De Consid.*, iv. 2.

difficulties for the good of others. The more pains they take in such meditation, the more clearly will priests understand the greatness, the excellence, the holiness of their office. They will see how sad it is that so many men, redeemed by Jesus Christ, should run headlong to eternal ruin; and by meditation upon the divine nature they will themselves be more strongly moved, and will more effectually excite others, to the love of God.

Virtuous nations rewarded with temporal prosperity.

Such, then, is the surest way to secure the general welfare. But let us not be frightened by the greatness of our difficulties, or despair of cure by reason of the long continuance of evil. The impartial and unchangeable justice of God reserves due reward for good deeds and fitting punishment for sin. But since the life of peoples and nations does not outlast this world, these necessarily receive their retribution upon this earth. Indeed, it is not a new thing for prosperity to have place in a sinful nation; and this by the just designs of God, Who from time to time rewards good deeds with prosperity, for no people is altogether without worth. This St. Augustine considered to have been the case with the Roman people. The law, nevertheless, remains clear: that nations may prosper, it is to the interest of all that virtue—and especially justice, the mother of all virtues—should be publicly practised. *Justice exalteth a nation; but sin maketh nations miserable.* * It is not our purpose here to consider how far evil deeds may succeed, or whether some kingdoms, while flourishing according to their desires, may nevertheless bear within them the seeds of ruin

---

* *Prov.* xiv. 34.

and misery. This one thing, of which history has innumerable examples, We wish to be understood, that injustice is always punished, and with greater severity the longer it has been continued. We, however, are greatly consoled by the words of the Apostle S. Paul: *For all things are yours; and you are Christ's, and Christ is God's.* * That is, by the hidden dispensation of divine Providence the course of earthly things is so guided and governed that all things that happen to man turn to the glory of God, and lead to the salvation of the true disciples of Jesus Christ. Of these the mother and sustainer, the leader and guardian, is the Church; which, united to Christ her spouse in intimate and unchangeable charity, is also joined to Him in common contest and in common conquest. Hence We are not, and cannot be, anxious for the sake of the Church; but We greatly fear for the salvation of very many who in their pride despise the Church, and by many kinds of error are borne along to their own destruction. We are anxious for those States which We cannot but see have turned from God, and are sleeping in the midst of danger with dull security and insensibility. " Nothing is equal in power to the Church . . . How many have opposed the Church and have themselves perished ! The Church reaches to the heavens. Such is the Church's greatness : she conquers when attacked; when beset by snares she triumphs ; . . . . she struggles, and is not overthrown; she fights, and is not overcome."†

Not only is she not conquered, but she preserves entire that reforming power and efficient principle

---

* 1 *Cor.* iii. 22, 23.   † S. John Chrysost.

The hope of the future is centred in the Church. of salvation which she derives unceasingly from God, and which remains unchanged by time. And, if by this power she freed the world grown old in vice and lost in superstition, why should she not by the same bring it back again to the right way? Let suspicion and enmity cease at length; let all obstacles be removed, and let the Church, whose duty it is to guard and spread abroad the benefits obtained by Jesus Christ, be restored everywhere to her rights. Then shall we know by experience how far the light of the Gospel can reach, and what the power of Christ our Redeemer can effect.

A prayer for the well-being of the Church. This year, now coming to a close, has given, as We have said, many signs of a reviving faith. Would that this little spark may increase till it becomes a mighty flame, which, burning up the roots of vice, may quickly prepare the way for the restoration of morals and for salutary works. We, indeed, who command the mystical barque of the Church in so formidable a storm, fix Our mind and heart upon the Divine Pilot Who sits unseen at the helm. Thou seest, O Lord, how the winds have burst forth from every side; how the sea rages, and the waves are lashed to fury. Command, we beseech Thee, Who alone canst do so, the winds and the sea. Give back to mankind that tranquillity of order, that true peace which the world cannot give. By Thy grace and impulse let men be restored to proper order, with piety towards God, with justice and love towards their neighbour, with temperance in regard to themselves, and with reason controlling all their passions. Let Thy kingdom come; let the duty of submitting to Thee and serving Thee be learnt by those who, far from Thee, seek truth and salvation with a purpose that is all vain. In Thy laws justice and a father's gentleness are found; and Thou grantest to us of Thy own good-will the power to keep Thy commands. The life of man on earth is a warfare, but Thou lookest down upon the struggle and helpest man to conquer; Thou raisest him that falls, and crownest him that triumphs."*

Our mind is upheld by these thoughts to a joyful and firm hope; and as a pledge of heavenly favours, and of our good-will, we most lovingly in the Lord grant to you, Venerable Brothers, and to the clergy and people of the whole Catholic world, the Apostolic Blessing.

---

* Cf. S. Aug. *in Ps.* 32.

CONCERNING MODERN ERRORS.

SOCIALISM, COMMUNISM, NIHILISM.

Encyclical Letter, December 28, 1878.

AS the nature of our Apostolic office required of Us, We have not omitted, from the very outset of Our Pontificate, addressing you, Venerable Brothers, in Encyclical Letters, in order to advert to the deadly plague which is tainting Society to its very core and bringing it to a state of extreme peril. At the same time we called attention to certain most effectual remedies, by which Society may be renewed unto salvation and enabled to escape the crisis now threatening.

The character and aims of certain sects are described. But the evils which We then deplored have taken in a brief space of time such wide-spread growth that We are compelled to address you anew, with the words of the prophet resounding as it were in our ears: *Cry, cease not, lift up thy voice like a trumpet.* *

You understand as a matter of course, Venerable Brothers, that we are alluding to that sect of men who, under the motley and all but barbarous terms and titles of Socialists, Communists and Nihilists, are spread abroad throughout the world and bound intimately together in baneful alliance, no longer look for strong support in secret meetings held in darksome

---
* *Isai.* lviii. i.

places, but standing forth openly and boldly in the light of day, strive to carry out the purpose, long resolved upon, of uprooting the foundations of civilised society at large.

These are they in very truth who, as the sacred text bears witness, *Defile the flesh, and despise dominion, and blaspheme majesty.* * They leave nothing scathless or uninjured of that which human and divine laws alike have wisely ordained to ensure the preservation and honour of life. From the Heads of States to whom, as the Apostle admonishes, all owe submission, and on whom the rights of authority are bestowed by God Himself, these sectaries withhold obedience, and preach up the perfect equality of all men in regard to rights alike and duties. The natural union of man and woman, which is held sacred even among barbarous nations, they hold in scorn; and its bond, whereby family life is chiefly maintained, they slacken, or else yield up to the sway of lust. In short, spurred on by greedy hankering after things present, which is *the root of all evils, which some coveting have erred from the faith,* † they attack the right of property, sanctioned by the law of nature,. and with signal depravity, while pretending to feel solicitous about the needs, and anxious to satisfy the requirements of all, they strain every effort to seize upon and hold in common all that has been individually acquired by title of lawful inheritance, through intellectual or manual labour, or economy in living. These monstrous views they proclaim in public meetings, uphold in booklets, and spread broadcast

They attack authority, the family, private property.

---

* *Jude* 8.   † 1 *Tim.* iv. 19.

everywhere through the daily press. Hence the hallowed dignity and authority of Rulers has incurred such odium on the part of rebellious subjects that evil-minded traitors, spurning all control have, many a time within a recent period boldly raised impious hands against even the very Heads of States.

The source of this rationalism, which since the 16th century has invaded the political, scientific, and economical order.

Such daring conduct on the part of disloyal individuals, which threatens the civilised community from day to day with even graver perils, and troubles the mind of all with anxious fears, draws its cause and origin from those venomous teachings which, like pernicious seed scattered far and wide among the nations, have produced in course of time death-bearing fruit. In fact, Venerable Brothers, you know full well that the atrocious war which, starting from the sixteenth century, was declared against the Catholic Faith by the Reformers, and which has been growing amain from day to day in vehemence, aimed at giving free course to the rejection of all revelation, the subversion of the supernatural order, and the enthronement of unaided reason, with its vagaries or rather ravings. Deriving pretentiously its name from Reason, this false doctrine, by flattering and stimulating the eagerness to outstrip others which is interwoven with man's nature, and giving the rein to every kind of unlawful desire, has taken willing possession of the minds of great numbers, and has even pervaded the whole of civilised society. Hence by a fresh act of impiety, unknown even to very Pagans, governments have been organised without God and the order established by Him being taken at all into account. It has even been contended that public authority, with its dignity and its power of ruling, originates not from God but from the mass of the people, which, considering itself unfettered by all divine sanction, refuses to submit to any laws that it has not itself passed of its own free will. Next, after having attacked and cast away the supernatural truths of faith as being contrary to reason, the very Author and Redeemer of mankind has been forced slowly and gradually to withdraw from the scheme of studies at universities, colleges and high schools, as well as from all the practical working of public life. In fine, after having consigned to oblivion the rewards and punishments of a future and never-ending existence, the keen longing after happiness has been narrowed down to the range of the present life. With such doctrines spread far and wide, and such licence in thought and action, it is no wonder that men of the most lowly condition, heart-sick of a humble home or poor workshop should fix eager eyes on the abodes and fortunes of the wealthy; no wonder that tranquillity no longer prevails in public or private life, or that the human race has been hurried onward to well-nigh the verge of ruin.

But the supreme pastors of the Church, on whom devolves the charge of guarding the Lord's flock from the snares of the enemy, have in good time devoted their energies to avert the danger impending, and to provide for the safety of the faithful. In fact, as soon as secret societies began to take extension, in the midst whereof the germs of those evil principles already adverted to, were nursed, the Roman Pontiffs Clement XV.

The care taken by the Popes to ward off danger by excommunicating members of Secret Societies.

and Benedict XIV. failed not to unmask the impious designs of the sectaries, and to warn the faithful throughout the world concerning the mischiefs they were thus hatching in secret. But when by those who gloried in the title of "philosophers," a certain unbridled liberty was assigned to man, and the "new law," as they term it, began in opposition to the divine and natural law to be set forth and gather sanction, Pius VI., of happy memory, forthwith laid bare by public documents the pernicious character and falsity of those principles, and at the same time, with apostolic foresight, predicted the utter ruin to which the deluded multitudes were being hurried. But since, notwithstanding the measures resorted to, none proved of avail to prevent their wicked doctrines from day by day gaining ground with the people, and obtaining ascendancy even in public decisions of government, Popes Pius VII. and Leo XII. excommunicated secret societies, and once more gave warning to society of the perils that threatened it. In fine, the world at large is fully aware in what earnest terms, and with what resoluteness of soul and unflinching constancy, Our glorious predecessor, Pius IX., of happy memory, by Allocutions alike and Encyclical Letters addressed to the Bishops of the whole world, levied war against the iniquitous endeavours of these sects, and furthermore even denounced by name the plague of Socialism thence bursting forth.

It is to be deplored, however, that they to whom has been entrusted the care of the common welfare,

The Gospel teachings opposed to Socialism. allowing themselves to be circumvented by the fraudulent devices of infamous men and terror-stricken at their threats, have ever displayed towards the Church feelings of suspicion or even of hostility, not understanding that the endeavours of these sects would have been of no effect had the doctrine of the Catholic Church and the authority of the Roman Pontiffs, among Rulers and peoples alike, always remained in due honour. For the *Church of the living God, which is the pillar and ground of truth*,* proclaims those doctrines and precepts whereby the security and calm of Society is provided for, and the accursed brood of Socialism is utterly destroyed.

For although the Socialists, turning to evil use the Gospel itself so as to deceive more readily the unwary, have been wont to twist it to their meaning, so still striking is the disagreement between their criminal teachings and the pure doctrine of Christ, that no greater can exist: *For what participation hath justice with injustice, or what fellowship hath light with darkness?*† They in good sooth cease not from asserting—as we have already mentioned—that all men are by nature equal, and hence they contend that neither honour nor respect is owed to public authority, nor any obedience to the laws, saving perhaps to those which have been sanctioned according to their good pleasure. Contrariwise, from the Gospel records, equality among men consists in this, that one and all, possessing the same nature, are called to the sublime dignity of being sons of God; and, moreover, that one and the same end being set before all, each and every one has

---
* 1 *Tim.* iii. 15. † 2 *Cor.* vi. 14.

to be judged according to the same laws and to have punishments or rewards meted out according to individual deserts. There is however an inequality of right and authority which emanates from the Author of nature Himself, *of whom all paternity in Heaven and earth is named.* * As regards Rulers and subjects, all without exception, according to Catholic teaching and precept, are mutually bound by duties and rights, in such manner that, on the one hand, moderation is enjoined on the appetite for power, and, on the other, obedience is shown to be easy, stable and wholly honourable. Therefore does the Church constantly urge upon each and all who are subject to her the apostolic precept: *There is no power but from God; and those that are, are ordained of God. Therefore he that resisteth the powers resisteth the ordinance of God. And they that resist, purchase to themselves damnation.* And again: *Be subject of necessity, not only for wrath, but also for conscience' sake; and render to all men their dues. Tribute, to whom tribute is due; custom to whom custom; fear to whom fear; honour to whom honour.* † For He who has created and governs all things, has in His provident wisdom so disposed them that the lowest attain to their end by the middlemost, and the middlemost by the highest. Just then as the Almighty willed that, in the heavenly kingdom itself, the choirs of angels should be of differing ranks, subordinated the one to the other; again just as in the Church God has established different grades of orders with diversity of functions, so that all should not be *Apostles, all not Doctors, all not Prophets;* ‡

The Church inculcates obedience of subjects to Rulers;

---
* *Eph.* iii. 15.   † *Rom.* xiii. 1-7.   ‡ 1 *Cor.* xii. 29.

so also has He established in Civil Society many orders of varying dignity, right and power. And this, to the end that the State, like the Church, should form one body comprising many members, some excelling others in rank and importance, but all alike necessary to one another and solicitous for the common welfare.

and moderation to the Rulers of the people. But to the end that the Rulers of the people shall employ the power bestowed for the advancement, and not detriment, of those under rule, the Church of Christ very fittingly warns the Rulers themselves that the Sovereign Judge will call them to a strict and speedy account, and evoking the words of Divine wisdom, she addresses them one and all in God's name. *Give ear, you that rule the people, and that please yourselves in multitudes of nations; for power is given you by the Lord, and strength by the most High, Who will examine your works, and search out your thoughts; . . . . for a most severe judgment shall be for them that bear rule. . . . For God will not accept any man's person, neither will He stand in awe of any one's greatness: for He hath made the little and the great, and He hath equally care of all. But a greater punishment is ready for the more mighty.** Should it, however, happen, at any time, that in the public exercise of authority Rulers act rashly and arbitrarily, the teaching of the Catholic Church does not allow subjects to rise against them, without further warranty, lest peace and order become more and more disturbed, and Society run the risk of greater detriment. And when things have come to such a pass as to hold out no further

---
* *Wisd.* vi. 3. seqq.

hope, she teaches that a remedy is to be sought in the virtue of Christian patience and in urgent prayer to God. But should it please legislators and Rulers to enjoin or sanction anything repugnant to the divine and natural law, the dignity and duty of the name of Christian and the Apostolic injunction proclaim that one *ought to obey God rather than men.* *

Moreover, the salutary influence of the Church, which redounds to the upholding of well-regulated order in Civil Society and promotes its conservation, the family circle itself (which is the starting-point of every city and every State) necessarily feels and experiences. For you are fully aware, Venerable Brothers, that the governing principle of family life has, in accordance with the requirements of natural law, its basis in the indissoluble union of husband and wife, and its superstructure in the duties and rights of parents and children, and of masters and servants towards each other. You are further aware that the theories of Socialism would quickly destroy this family life, since the stability afforded by marriage under religious sanction once lost, paternal authority over children and the duties of children to parents are necessarily and most harmfully slackened. Contrariwise, *marriage, honourable to all,* † which from the beginning of the world God Himself instituted for the propagation and preservation of the human race, and decreed to be indissoluble, the Church holds to have become more stable and holy through Christ, Who conferred on it the dignity of a sacrament, and willed

The Church defends the indissoluble union of husband and wife.

---
* *Acts* v. 29.   † *Heb.* xiii. 4.

to make it an image of His own union with the Church. Wherefore, as the Apostle admonishes: *As Christ is the head of the Church,* so is *the husband the head of the wife:** and just as the Church is subject to Christ, Who cherishes it with most chaste and lasting love, so is it becoming that women also should be subject to their husbands, and by them in turn be loved with faithful and constant affection.

<small>The Church defines the right and duties of parents and children, and of masters and servants.</small>

In like manner the Church regulates the authority of the father and the master in such mode as to keep children and servants within their duty, without however allowing authority to be overstepped. For, according to Catholic teaching, the authority of the heavenly Father and Lord flows forth upon parents and masters, and on that account receives not only its origin and power from God, but also its very nature and character. Hence does the Apostle exhort children to *obey their parents in the Lord, and to honour their father and their mother, which is the first commandment with a promise.*† *And you, fathers, provoke not your children to anger, but bring them up in the discipline and correction of the Lord.*‡ And again by the same divine Apostolic injunction it is urged on servants and masters that the former *should obey their masters according to the flesh . . . as to Christ . . . . . with a good will serving as to the Lord. . . .* but the latter should *forbear threatenings, knowing that the Lord of all is in heaven, and there is no respect of persons with Him.*‡ Were all these things observed

---

* *Eph.* v. 23. † *Eph.* vi. 1, 2. ‡ Ibid. v. 4. § Ibid. vi. 5, 6, 7.

by every one whom they concern, according to the intent of the Divine Will, each family would truly present a likeness of the heavenly home, and the wondrous benefits thence resulting would not be limited simply to the family circle, but would spread abroad abundantly over the State at large.

As regards the maintenance of public and private tranquillity, Catholic wisdom, sustained by both divine and natural law, prudently provides, through what it holds and teaches touching the right of ownership and the apportioning of personal property which has been accumulated for the wants and requirements of life. For the Socialists wrongly assume the right of property to be of mere human invention, repugnant to the natural equality between men; and, preaching up the community of goods, declare that no one should endure poverty meekly, and that all may with impunity seize upon the possessions and usurp the rights of the wealthy. More wisely and profitably the Church recognises the existence of inequality amongst men, who are by nature unlike in mental endowment and strength of body, and even in amount of fortune; and she enjoins that the right of property and of its disposal, derived from nature, should in the case of every individual remain intact and inviolate. She knows full well indeed that robbery and rapine have been so forbidden by God, the Author and Protector of every right, that it is unlawful even to covet the goods of others, and that thieves and robbers no less than adulterers and idolaters are excluded from the

It acknowledges the rights of possessing and disposing of private property, honours and relieves the poor, enjoins the rich to give alms.

kingdom of Heaven. Nor does she, on this account, loving Mother as she is, omit solicitude for the poor, or fail to provide for their needs; nay, taking them to her arms with maternal affection, and knowing that they in a manner represent the person of Christ Himself, Who accounts as done unto Him any benefit conferred upon the lowliest among the poor, she holds them in great account, brings them aid to the utmost of her power, takes thought to have erected in every land in their behoof Homes and Refuges where they can be received, nurtured, and tended; and takes these charitable foundations under her protecting care. Moreover, she lays the rich under strict command to give of their superfluity to the poor, impressing them with fear of the divine judgment which will exact the penalty of eternal punishment unless they succour the wants of the needy. In fine, she cheers and comforts exceedingly the hearts of the poor, either by setting before them the example of Christ, Who, *being rich became poor for our sakes;* * or by reminding them of the words by which Jesus pronounced the poor to be *blessed*, and enjoined them to hope for the reward of eternal bliss. Who then does not perceive that herein lies the best means of appeasing the undying conflict between the rich and poor? For, as the evidence of things and facts clearly demonstrates, if such conclusion be disallowed or made light of, it must come about either that the vast majority of mankind will fall back into that most abject condition of bondage, which through a long lapse of time obtained amongst pagan nations, or

---

* 2 *Cor.* viii. 9.

else that human society will be agitated by constant outbreaks and ravaged by plunder and rapine, such as even of late years we have had occasion to deplore.

Since things have come to this pass, Venerable Brothers, We, on whom is laid the charge of governing the Universal Church, pointed out even at the very outset of our Pontificate to the nations and their Rulers, tossed about by so dire a tempest, the port to which they could betake themselves in all safety. And now, moved greatly by the extreme peril which actually threatens, We lift up anew Our Apostolic voice, and conjure them again and again, for the sake of their own safety and that of the State, to welcome and obey the teaching of that Church which has deserved so well in promoting the public prosperity of nations, and to recognise once for all that the relations of the State and of Religion are so bound together as that whatever is withdrawn from religion, impairs by so much the dutiful submission of the subject and the dignity of authority. And when they shall have recognised that the Church of Christ is possessed of a power to stave off the pest of Socialism, too mighty to be found in human enactments or in the strong hand of the civil power or in military force, let them re-establish that Church in the condition and liberty needed in order to be able to exercise her most salutary influence for the good of society in general. Do you, however, Venerable Brothers, who have keen insight as to the nature and origin of the ills thickening ever in the world, apply yourselves with all zeal and energy

An appeal to Peoples and Rulers to hearken to the voice of the Church teaching, and to restore liberty to her.

CONCERNING MODERN ERRORS. 239

Appeal to Pastors to plant deep down in the souls of the faithful the teaching of the Church;

of spirit to inculcate Catholic Doctrine, that it may reach and strike deep root in the souls of all. Provide as far as may be that from early years all may grow accustomed to cherish a filial love towards God, and to revere His sovereign sway; to show due submission to Rulers and the laws, to bridle their passions, and zealously uphold the authority which God has established alike in the State and in the family circle. Moreover it behoves you to strive earnestly that the children of the Catholic Church venture not to lend their name, nor in any way to give countenance to this hateful sect, but on the contrary that by worthy deeds and honourable line of action in all particulars, they show how well and happily human society would prosper were the individual members distinguishable for the regularity of their conduct and for their virtuous life. Finally, as the confederates of Socialism are sought mainly among those who occupy themselves in business pursuits, or give themselves to manual labour, and who, wearied out by sheer hard work, are more easily entrapped by the hope of wealth and promise of prosperity, it seems expedient to encourage Associations for handicraftsmen and labouring men, which, placed under the sheltering care of religion, may render the members content with their lot and resigned to toil, inducing them to lead a peaceful and tranquil life.

and to establish Associations of working men.

On Our undertakings, Venerable Brothers, and on yours, may He confer favouring aid to Whom we are bound to refer the beginning and the end of all good.

We have ample ground to hope for speedy help during these auspicious days when the festival of Our Lord's Nativity is being celebrated. That new deliverance which Christ, born into a world sinking with years and well-nigh crushed with the weight of ills, charges us to hope for; that peace which then He announced to men through the ministry of Angels, He has promised to bestow likewise on us. For *the hand of the Lord is not shortened, that He cannot save, neither is His ear heavy, that it cannot hear.** During these days then of most happy augury, Venerable Brothers, wishing to you and to all the faithful of your Churches all joy and prosperity, We earnestly pray the Giver of all good gifts that anew to men may appear *the goodness and kindness of God our Saviour;* † Who, after having snatched us from the power of a ruthless enemy, has raised us up to the most exalted dignity of being sons of God. And in order that Our vows may be the more speedily and abundantly satisfied, join with us, Venerable Brothers, in addressing to God fervent prayers, invoking also the patronage of the Blessed Virgin Mary, ever-immaculate, and of her spouse, Joseph, as also of the blessed Apostles, Peter and Paul, in whose intercession We greatly confide. And in the meantime, with inmost affection of heart to you, Venerable Brothers, to your Clergy and to all the faithful throughout the world, as a harbinger of the divine gifts, We impart Our Apostolic Blessing.

Hope of Divine aid.

---

* *Is.* lix. 1.   † *Tit.* iii. 4.

WORKING-MEN'S CLUBS
AND ASSOCIATIONS.

(Address to the Officials and Members of the Societies for the Furtherance of Catholic Interests amongst the Industrial Classes in France, February 24, 1885.)

Catholic Working-men's Associations.

IT is with special satisfaction, dearly beloved Children, that We approve the profoundly Christian sentiments which you have just expressed to Us. We rejoice greatly at this fresh manifestation of faith on the part of the Catholic Associations of France, and notably of the zealous work of the Catholic Working-men's Clubs, of which at the time being you are the representatives. This organisation is worthy of all praise, and We cannot but commend highly the thought which prompted you to set it on foot. Alarmed at the discords and confusion engendered both in principles and conduct through the spread of revolutionary doctrines, you have set your minds on studying, by the light of Christian teaching, the great social truths, and on propagating them, more especially among the industrial classes. You have assured yourselves that the ills which afflict the majority of families belonging to those classes are due chiefly to the abandonment of religious practices and to the influence of evil tenets. And you know from experience, that the labouring-man who no longer finds in religion the stay and consolation of which he, more than any other, stands in need, in order to support the painful difficulties and troubles of his less wealthy position, will seek his satisfaction in the lowest enjoyments and will give free course to his vilest passions, to the detriment of his own moral good and to the great peril of society at large.

We congratulate you, therefore, dearly beloved Children, upon the generous efforts you are unceasingly making to lead back to Christian principles the numerous families engaged in industrial pursuits, and We hail with satisfaction the cheering results hitherto obtained.

Self-seeking Agitators. Continue to develop them more and more for the greater good of all, but most of all for the benefit of workingmen. Agitators are aiming at making use of the labouring classes as instruments whereby to satisfy their own ambition. They delude them by empty promises; flatter them by proclaiming loudly their rights, without referring ever to their duties; they enkindle in their minds a hatred of land-owners and of the wealthy classes; and at length, so soon as they deem the moment favourable for their harmful purposes, they launch them into perilous enterprises wherein none but the ringleaders reap advantage.

Not thus does the Church of Jesus Christ act. Like a loving mother devoid of all self-seeking, she is solely solicitous for, and yearns after the happiness of her children; she applies to their ills the only saving remedies; for she alone knows the secret of how to solve the difficult social problems that are agitating the world. We ourselves, in manifold circumstances, have pointed out

The Church and social ills.

those remedies. We have exhorted the Catholic Faithful of all countries to revive anew the wise Institutions or Corporations of Working-men, which, in better times, have flourished under the inspiring influence of the Church, to the great advantage, spiritual alike and temporal, of the poor and labouring classes. Besides facilitating the fulfilment of the duties of Christian piety, these Institutions assure to the working-man the education and suitable training of his children, assistance and charitable aid in case of sickness or distress, and support in old age. They implant love in the heart of all, instead of hate, which but too often separates the employed from their employers. As regards the working-men they inspire them with respect and obedience, and loyalty and devotedness in their toil; and they remind employers of labour that Christians of every class are their brothers in Jesus Christ; that justice should preside over all their acts; that charity and gentleness should attemper both command and correction.

Thanks to the influence of such salutary Institutions we should soon see brought to an end that fratricidal conflict of which you were so lately speaking, and which, wholly unknown in the ages of faith, exercises in the present day such baneful ravages.

So far as you are concerned, dearly-beloved Children, you have obeyed Our fatherly exhortations by forming religious Associations in the very midst of your industrial establishments. You have moreover clearly understood that, in order to ensure the success and stability of your charitable organizations, it was needful to let yourselves be guided by the pastors appointed for the governance of your respective dioceses. Following your example, We fondly hope that all Catholics of influence may sink party differences, which are a source of weakness, seek to join hands in a spirit of union, to work together harmoniously, to apply and develop Christian principles throughout all classes of society, and more especially to uphold good works on behalf of the labouring classes, and all those whose aim and purpose is to foster among the people the religious training of youth.

<small>United action for religious and social ends.</small>

That will doubtless prove one of the surest and most efficacious means to heal the ills of the present time and to prepare for the Church and for civil society a better future. In that view and to strengthen your courage, dearly-beloved Children, We are happy to satisfy the desire which has brought you together around Us to-day, and We accord with all Our heart, to yourselves, to your families, to the several Heads of industrial works whose delegates you are, and to all the working-men who are members of your pious Societies, the Apostolic Benediction.

THE REUNION OF CHRISTENDOM.

Encyclical Letter, June 20, 1894.

THE splendid tokens of public rejoicing which have come to Us from all sides in the whole course of last year, to commemorate Our Episcopal Jubilee, and which were lately crowned by the remarkable devotion of the Spanish nation, have afforded Us special joy, inasmuch as the unity of the Church and the admirable adhesion of her members to the Sovereign Pontiff have shone forth in this perfect agreement of concurring sentiments. During those days it seemed as if the Catholic world, forgetful of everything else, had centred its gaze and all its thoughts upon the Vatican.

The Pope's Jubilee, and unity amongst Catholics. The special missions sent by kings and princes, the many pilgrimages, the letters We received so full of affectionate feeling, the sacred services—everything clearly brought out the fact that all Catholics are of one mind and of one heart in their veneration for the Apostolic See. And this was all the more pleasing and agreeable to Us, that it is entirely in conformity with Our intent and with Our endeavours. For, indeed, well acquainted with Our times, and mindful of the duties of Our ministry, We have constantly sought during the whole course of Our Pontificate, and striven, as far as it was possible, by teaching and action, to bind every nation and people more closely to us, and make manifest everywhere the salutary influence of the See of Rome. Therefore do We most earnestly offer thanks in the first place to the goodness of God, by Whose help and bounty We have been preserved to attain Our great age; and then, next, to all the princes and rulers, to the bishops and clergy, and to as many as have co-operated by such repeated tokens of piety and reverence, to honour Our character and office, while affording Us personally such seasonable consolation.

A great multitude outside Catholic Unity. A great deal, however, has been wanting to the entire fulness of that consolation. Amidst these very manifestations of public joy and reverence Our thoughts went out towards the immense multitude of those who were strangers to the gladness that filled all Catholic hearts: some because they lie in absolute ignorance of the Gospel; others because they dissent from the Catholic belief, though they bear the name of Christians.

This thought has been, and is, a source of deep concern to Us; for it is impossible to think of such a large portion of mankind, deviating, as it were, from the right path, as they move away from Us, and not experience a sentiment of innermost grief.

The Holy Father's concern for those outside Catholic Unity. But since We hold upon this earth the place of God Almighty, Who will have all men to be saved and to come to the knowledge of the truth, and now that Our advanced age and the bitterness of anxious cares urge Us on towards the end common to every mortal, We feel drawn to follow the example of Our Redeemer and Master Jesus Christ, Who, when about to return to Heaven, implored of God, His Father, in earnest prayer, that His disciples and followers should be of one mind and of one heart: *I pray . . . that they all may be one, as Thou Father in Me, and I in Thee: that they also may be one in Us.* And as this Divine prayer and supplication does not include only the souls who then believed in Jesus Christ, but also every one of those who were henceforth to believe in Him, this prayer holds out to Us no indifferent reason for confidently expressing Our hopes, and for making all possible endeavours, in order that the men of every race and clime should be called and moved to embrace the unity of Divine faith.

<small>The most unfortunate of all nations.</small> Pressed on to Our intent by charity, that hastens fastest there where the need is greatest, We direct Our first thoughts to those most unfortunate of all nations who have never received the light of the Gospel, or who, after having possessed it, have lost it through neglect or the vicissitudes of time: hence do they ignore God, and live in the depths of error. Now, as all salvation comes from Jesus Christ—*for there is no other name under Heaven given to men whereby we must be saved*—Our ardent desire is that the most holy Name of Jesus should rapidly pervade and fill every land.

And here, indeed, is a duty which the Church, faithful to the Divine mission entrusted to her, has never neglected. What has been the object of her labours for more than nineteen centuries? Is there any other work she has undertaken with greater zeal and constancy than that of bringing the nations of the earth to the truth and principles of Christianity? To-day, as ever, by Our authority, the heralds of the Gospel constantly cross the seas to reach the farthest corners of the earth; and We pray God daily that in His goodness He may deign to increase the number of His ministers who are really worthy of this Apostolate, and who are ready to sacrifice their convenience, their health, and their very life, if need be, in order to extend the frontiers of the kingdom of Christ.

Do Thou, above all, O Saviour and Father of mankind, Christ Jesus, hasten and do not delay to bring about what Thou didst once promise to do—that when lifted up from the earth Thou wouldst draw all things to Thyself. Come then, at last, and manifest Thyself to the immense multitude of souls who have not felt, as yet, the ineffable blessings which Thou hast earned for men with Thy blood; rouse those who are sitting in darkness, and in the shadow of death, that, enlightened by the rays of Thy wisdom and virtue, in Thee and by Thee "they may be made perfect in one."

Former unity amongst civilised nations. As We consider the mystery of this unity We see before Us all the countries which have long since passed, by the mercy of God, from time-worn error to the wisdom of the Gospel. Nor could We, indeed, recall anything more pleasing or better calculated to extol the work of Divine Providence, than the memory of the days of yore, when the Faith that had come down from Heaven was looked upon as the common inheritance of one and all; when civilised nations, separated by distance, character, and habits, in spite of frequent disagreements and warfare on other points, were united by Christian faith in all that concerned religion. The recollection of that time causes Us to regret all the more deeply that, as the ages rolled by, the waves of suspicion and hatred arose, and great and flourishing nations were dragged away, in an evil hour, from the bosom of the Roman Church. In spite of that, however, We trust in the mercy of God's Almighty power, in Him Who alone can fix the hour of His benefits and Who has power to incline man's will as He pleases; and We turn to those same nations, exhorting and beseeching them with fatherly love to put an end to their dissensions and return again to unity.

The Eastern Churches. First of all, then, We cast an affectionate look upon the East, from whence in the beginning came forth the salvation of the world. Yes, and the yearning desire of Our heart bids Us conceive the hope that the day is not far distant, when the Eastern Churches, so illustrious in their ancient faith and glorious past, will return to the fold they have abandoned. We hope it, all the more, that the distance separating them from us is not so great: nay, with some few exceptions, we agree so entirely on other heads that, in defence of the Catholic faith, we often have recourse to reasons and testimony borrowed from the teaching, the rites, and customs of the East.

The principal subject of contention is the primacy of

the Roman Pontiff. But let them look back to the early years of their existence, let them consider the sentiments entertained by their forefathers, and examine what the oldest traditions testify, and it will, indeed, become evident to them that Christ's Divine utterance, *Thou art Peter, and upon this rock I will build My Church*, has undoubtedly been realised in the Roman Pontiffs. Many of these latter in the first ages of the Church were chosen from the East, and foremost among them, Anacletus, Evaristus, Anicetus, Eleutherius, Zosimus, and Agatho; and of these a great number, after governing the Church in wisdom and sanctity, consecrated their ministry with the shedding of their blood. The time, the reasons, the promoters of the unfortunate division, are well known. Before the day when man separated what God had joined together, the name of the Apostolic See was held in reverence by all the nations of the Christian world : and the East, like the West, agreed without hesitation in its obedience to the Pontiff of Rome, as the legitimate successor of St. Peter, and, therefore, the Vicar of Christ here on earth.

And, accordingly, if we refer to the beginning of the dissension, we shall see that Photius himself was careful to send his advocates to Rome on the matters that concerned him; and Pope Nicolas I. sent his legates to Constantinople from the Eternal City, without the slightest opposition, "in order to examine the case of Ignatius the Patriarch with all diligence, and to bring back to the Apostolic See a full and accurate report;" so that the history of the whole negotiation is a manifest confirmation of the primacy of the Roman See with which the dissension then began. Finally, in two great Councils, the second of Lyons and that of Florence, Latins and Greeks, as is notorious, easily agreed, and all unanimously proclaimed as dogma the supreme power of the Roman Pontiffs.

Appeal to the Easterns.
We have recalled these things intentionally, for they constitute an invitation to peace and reconciliation; and with all the more reason that in Our own days it would seem as if there were a more conciliatory spirit towards Catholics on the part of the Eastern Churches, and even some degree of kindly feeling. To mention an instance, those sentiments were lately made manifest when some of Our Faithful travelled to the East on a holy enterprise, and received so many proofs of courtesy and good will.

Therefore *Our mouth is open to you*, to you all of Greek or other Oriental Rites who are separated from the Catholic Church. We earnestly desire that each and every one of you should meditate upon the words, so full of gravity and love, addressed by Bessarion to your forefathers: " What answer shall we give to God when He comes to ask why we have separated from our brethren : to Him Who, to unite us and bring us into one fold, came down from heaven, was incarnate, and was crucified? What will our defence be in the eyes of posterity? Oh, my venerable Fathers, we must not suffer this to be, we must not entertain this thought, we must not thus so ill provide for ourselves and for our brethren."

Weigh carefully in your minds and before God the

nature of Our request. It is not for any human motive, but impelled by Divine charity and a desire for the salvation of all, that We advise the reconciliation and union with the Church of Rome; and We mean a perfect and complete union, such as could not subsist in any way if nothing else was brought about but a certain kind of agreement in the tenets of belief and an intercourse of fraternal love. The true union between Christians is that which Jesus Christ, the Author of the Church, instituted and desired, and which consists in a unity of faith and a unity of government.

Nor is there any reason for you to fear on that account, that We or any of Our successors will ever diminish your rights, the privileges of your patriarchs, or the established ritual of any one of your Churches. It has been and always will be the intent and tradition of the Apostolic See, to make a large allowance, in all that is right and good, for the primitive traditions and special customs of every nation. On the contrary, if you re-establish union with Us, you will see how, by God's bounty, the glory and dignity of your Churches will be remarkably increased. May God, then, in His goodness, hear the prayer that you yourselves address to Him: "Make the schisms of the Churches cease," and "Assemble those who are dispersed, bring back those who err, and unite them to Thy Holy Catholic and Apostolic Church." May you thus return to that one holy Faith which has been handed down both to Us and to you from time immemorial; which your forefathers preserved untainted, and which was enhanced by the rival splendour of the virtues, the great genius, and the sublime learning of St. Athanasius and St. Basil, St. Gregory of Nazianzum and St. John Chrysostom, the two Saints who bore the name of Cyril, and so many other great men whose glory belongs as a common inheritance to the East and to the West.

Appeal to the Slavs. Suffer that We should address you more particularly, nations of the Slavonic race, you whose glorious name and deeds are attested by many an ancient record. You know full well how much the Slavs are indebted to the merits of St. Cyril and St. Methodius, to whose memory We Ourselves rendered due honour only a few years ago. Their virtues and their labours were to great numbers of your race the source of civilization and salvation. And hence the admirable interchange, which existed for so long between the Slavonic nations and the Pontiffs of Rome, of favours on the one side and of filial devotion on the other. If in unhappy times many of your forefathers were separated from the Faith of Rome, consider now what priceless benefits a return of unity would bring to you. The Church is anxious to welcome you also to her arms, that she may give you manifold aids to salvation, prosperity, and grandeur.

Nations more recently separated. With no less affection do We now look upon the nations who, at a more recent date, were separated from the Roman Church by an extraordinary revolution of things and circumstances. Let them forget the various events of times gone by, let them raise their thoughts far above all that is human, and seeking only truth and salvation, reflect within their hearts upon the Church as it was constituted by Christ. If they will but compare that Church with their own communions, and consider what the actual state of religion is in these, they will easily acknowledge that, forgetful of their early history, they have drifted away, on many and important points, into the novelty of various errors; nor will they deny that of what may be called the patrimony of truth, which the authors of those innovations carried away with them in their desertion, there now scarcely remains to them any article of belief that is really certain and supported by authority.

Drifting into various errors. Nay, more, things have already come to such a pass that many do not even hesitate to root up the very foundation upon which alone rests all religion, and the hope of men, to wit, the Divine Nature of Jesus Christ, our Saviour. And again, whereas formerly they used to assert that the books of the Old and New Testament were written under the inspiration of God, they now deny them that authority: this, indeed, was an inevitable consequence when they granted to all the right of private interpretation. Hence, too, the acceptance of individual conscience as the sole guide and rule of conduct to the exclusion of any other: hence those conflicting opinions and numerous sects that fall away so often into the doctrines of Naturalism and Rationalism.

Therefore is it, that having lost all hope of an agreement in their persuasions, they now proclaim and recommend a union of brotherly love. And rightly too, no doubt, for we should all be united by the bond of mutual charity. Our Lord Jesus Christ enjoined it most emphatically, and wished that this love of one another should be the mark of His disciples. But how can hearts be united in perfect charity where minds do not agree in faith?

Catholic Unity the sure way of salvation. It is on this account that many of those We allude to, men of sound judgment and seeking after truth, have looked to the Catholic Church for the sure way of salvation; for they clearly understand that they could never be united to Jesus Christ as their head if they were not members of His body, which is the Church; nor really acquire the true Christian faith if they rejected the legitimate teaching confided to Peter and his successors. Such men as these have recognised in the Church of Rome the form and image of the true Church, which is clearly made manifest by the marks that God, her Author, placed upon her: and not a few who were possessed with penetrating judgment and a special talent for historical research, have shown forth in their remarkable writings the uninterrupted succession of the Church of Rome from the Apostles, the integrity of her doctrine, and the consistency of her rule and discipline.

With the example of such men before you, Our heart appeals to you even more than Our words: to you, Our Brethren, who for three centuries and more differ from Us on Christian faith; and to you all likewise, who in later times, for any reason whatsoever, have turned away from Us: *Let us all meet in the unity of faith and of the knowledge of the Son of God.* Suffer that We should invite you to the unity which has ever existed in the Catholic Church and can never fail; suffer that We should lovingly hold out Our hand to you. The Church, as the common mother of all, has long been calling you back to her; the Catholics of the world await you with brotherly love, that you may render holy worship to God together with Us, united in perfect charity by the profession of one Gospel, one faith, and one hope.

Exhortations to Catholics. To complete the harmony of this most desired unity, it remains for Us to address all those throughout the world whose salvation has long been the object of Our thoughts and watchful cares; We mean Catholics, whom the profession of the Roman faith, while it renders them obedient to the Apostolic See, preserves in union with Jesus Christ. There is no need to exhort them to true and holy unity, since through the Divine goodness they already possess it; nevertheless, they must be admonished, lest under pressure of the growing perils on all sides around them, through negligence or indolence they should lose this great blessing of God. For this purpose, let them take their rule of thought and action, as the occasion may require, from those instructions which at other times We have addressed to Catholic peoples, either collectively or individually; and above all, let them lay down for themselves as a supreme law, to yield obedience in all things to the teaching and authority of the Church, in no narrow or mistrustful spirit, but with their whole soul and promptitude of will.

On this account let them consider how injurious to Christian unity is that error, which in various forms of opinion has ofttimes obscured, nay, even destroyed the true character and idea of the Church. For by the will and ordinance of God, its Founder, it is a society perfect in its kind, whose office and mission it is to school mankind in the precepts and teachings of the Gospel, and by safeguarding the integrity of moral and the exercise of Christian virtue, to lead men to that happiness which is held out to every one in Heaven. And since it is, as we have said, a perfect society, therefore it is endowed with a living power and efficacy which is not derived from any external source, but in virtue of the ordinance of God and its own constitution, inherent in its very nature; for the same reason it has an inborn power of making laws, and justice requires that in its exercise it should be dependent on no one; it must likewise have freedom in other matters appertaining to its rights.

But this freedom is not of a kind to occasion rivalry or envy, for the Church does not covet power, nor is she urged on by any selfish desire; but this one thing she does wish, this only does she seek, to preserve amongst men the duties which virtue imposes, and by this means and in this way to provide for their everlasting welfare. Therefore is she wont to be yielding and indulgent as a mother; yea, it not unfrequently happens that in making large concessions to the exigencies of States, she refrains from the exercise of her own rights, as the compacts often concluded with civil governments abundantly testify.

The Church and the Civil Power are distinct. Nothing is more foreign to her disposition than to encroach on the rights of Civil power; but the Civil

R

power in its turn must respect the rights of the Church, and beware of arrogating them in any degree to itself. Now, what is the ruling spirit of the times when actual events and circumstances are taken into account? No other than this: it has been the fashion to regard the Church with suspicion, to despise, and hate, and spitefully calumniate her; and, more intolerable still, men strive with might and main to bring her under the sway of Civil governments. Hence it is that her property has been plundered and her liberty curtailed: hence, again, that the training of her priesthood has been beset with difficulties; that laws of exceptional rigour have been passed against her clergy; that Religious Orders, those excellent safeguards of Christianity, have been suppressed and placed under a ban; in a word, the principles and practice of the regalists have been renewed with increased virulence.

Such a policy is a violation of the most sacred rights of the Church, and it breeds enormous evils to States, for the very reason that it is in open conflict with the purposes of God. When God, in His most wise providence, placed over human society both temporal and spiritual authority, He intended them to remain distinct indeed, but by no means disconnected and at war with each other. On the contrary, both the will of God and the common weal of human society imperatively require that the Civil power should be in accord with the ecclesiastical in its rule and administration.

Hence the State has its own peculiar rights and duties, the Church likewise has hers; but it is necessary that each should be united with the other in the bonds of concord. Thus will it come about that the close mutual relations of Church and State will be freed from the present turmoil, which for manifold reasons is ill-advised and most distressing to all well-disposed persons; furthermore, it will be brought to pass that, without confusion or separation of the peculiar interests of each, the people will *render to Cæsar the things that are Cæsar's, and to God the things that are God's.*

The evils of Freemasonry. There is likewise a great danger threatening unity on the part of that association which goes by the name of the Society of Freemasons, whose fatal influence for a long time past oppresses Catholic nations in particular. Favoured by the agitations of the times, and waxing insolent in its power and resources and success, it strains every nerve to consolidate its sway and enlarge its sphere. It has already sallied forth from its hiding-places, where it hatched its plots, into the throng of cities, and as if to defy the Almighty, has set up its throne in this very city of Rome, the capital of the Catholic world. But what is most disastrous is, that wherever it has set its foot it penetrates into all ranks and departments of the commonwealth, in the hope of obtaining at last supreme control. This is, indeed, a great calamity: for its depraved principles and iniquitous designs are well known. Under the pretence of vindicating the rights of man and of reconstituting society, it attacks Christianity; it rejects revealed doctrine, denounces practices of piety, the divine sacraments, and every sacred thing as superstition; it strives to eliminate the Christian character from marriage and the family and the education of youth, and from every form of instruction, whether public or private, and to root out from the minds of men all respect for authority, whether human or divine. On its own part, it preaches the worship of nature, and maintains that by the principles of nature are truth and probity and justice to be measured and regulated. In this way, as is quite evident, man is being driven to adopt customs and habits of life akin to those of the heathen, only more corrupt in proportion as the incentives to sin are more numerous.

Although We have spoken on this subject in the strongest terms before, yet We are led by Our Apostolic watchfulness to urge it once more, and We repeat Our warning again and again, that in face of such an eminent peril, no precaution, howsoever great, can be looked upon as sufficient. May God in His mercy bring to naught their impious designs; nevertheless, let all Christians know and understand that the shameful yoke of Freemasonry must be shaken off once and for all; and let them be the first to shake it off who are most galled by its oppression — the men of Italy and of France. With what weapons and by what method this may best be done We Ourselves have already pointed out: the victory cannot be doubtful to those who trust in that leader Whose divine words still remain in all their force: *I have overcome the world.*

Benefits of Unity.
Were this twofold danger averted, and government and states restored to the unity of faith, it is wonderful what efficacious

remedies for evils and abundant store of benefits would ensue. We will touch upon the principal ones.

The first regards the dignity and office of the Church. She would receive that honour which is her due, and she would go on her way, free from envy and strong in her liberty, as the minister of Gospel truth and grace to the notable welfare of States. For as she has been given by God as a teacher and guide to the human race, she can contribute assistance which is peculiarly adapted to direct even the most radical transformations of time to the common good, to solve the most complicated questions, and to promote uprightness and justice, which are the most solid foundations of the commonwealth.

Unity of Faith brings peace amongst nations. Moreover, there would be a marked increase of union among the nations, a thing most desirable to ward off the horrors of war.

We behold the condition of Europe. For many years past peace has been rather an appearance than a reality. Possessed with mutual suspicions, almost all the nations are vying with one another in equipping themselves with military armaments. Inexperienced youths are removed from parental direction and control, to be thrown amid the dangers of the soldier's life; robust young men are taken from agriculture, or ennobling studies, or trade, or the arts, to be put under arms. Hence, the treasures of States are exhausted by the enormous expenditure, the national resources are frittered away, and private fortunes impaired; and this, as it were, armed peace, which now prevails, cannot last much longer. Can this be the normal condition of human society? Yet we cannot escape from this situation, and obtain true peace, except by the aid of Jesus Christ. For to repress ambition and covetousness and envy—the chief instigators of war—nothing is more fitted than the Christian virtues and, in particular, the virtue of justice; for, by its exercise, both the law of nations and the faith of treaties may be maintained inviolate, and the bonds of brotherhood continue unbroken, if men are but convinced that *justice exalteth a nation.*

Christian virtues a guarantee of the common weal. As in its external relations, so in the internal life of the State itself, the Christian virtues will provide a guarantee of the common weal much more sure and stronger far than any which laws or armies can afford. For there is no one who does not see that the dangers to public security and order are daily on the increase, since seditious societies continue to conspire for the overthrow and ruin of States, as the frequency of their atrocious outrages testifies.

There are two questions, forsooth—the one called the *social*, the other the *political* question—which are discussed with the greatest vehemence. Both of them, without doubt, are of the last importance, and, though praiseworthy efforts have been put forth, in studies, and measures, and experiments, for their wise and just solution, yet nothing could contribute more to this purpose than that the minds of men in general should be imbued with right sentiments of duty from the internal principle of Christian faith. We treated expressly of the social question, in this sense, a short time ago, from the standpoint of principles drawn from the Gospel and natural reason.

The Political Question. As regards the political question, which aims at reconciling liberty with authority—two things which many confound in theory, and separate too widely in practice— most efficient aid may be derived from Christian philosophy. For, when this point has been settled and recognised by common agreement, that whatsoever the form of government the authority is from God, reason at once perceives that in some there is a legitimate right to command, in others the corresponding duty to obey, and that without prejudice to their dignity, since obedience is rendered to God rather than to man; and God has denounced the most rigorous judgment against those in authority, if they fail to represent Him with uprightness and justice. Then the liberty of the individual can afford ground of suspicion or envy to no one; since, without injury to any, his conduct will be guided by truth and rectitude and whatever is allied to public order. Lastly, if it be considered what influence is possessed by the Church, the mother of and peacemaker between rulers and peoples, whose mission it is to help them both with her authority and counsel, then it will be most manifest how much it concerns the common weal that all nations should resolve to unite in the same belief and the same profession of the Christian faith.

A new order of things would arise from Unity. With these thoughts in Our mind and ardent yearnings in Our heart, We see from afar what would be the new order of things that would arise upon the earth, and nothing could be sweeter to Us than the contemplation of the benefits that would flow from it. It can hardly be imagined what immediate and rapid progress would be made all over the earth, in all manner of greatness and prosperity, with the establishment of tranquillity and peace, the promotion of studies, the founding and the multiplying on Christian lines according to our directions, of associations for the cultivators of the soil, for workmen and tradesmen, through whose agency rapacious usury would be put down, and a large field opened up for useful labours.

Unity would bring blessings to uncivilised nations.

And these abundant benefits would not be confined within the limits of civilised nations, but, like an overcharged river, would flow far and wide. It must be remembered, as We observed at the outset, that an immense number of races have been waiting, all through the long ages, to receive the light of truth and civilisation. Most certainly, the counsels of God with regard to the eternal salvation of peoples are far removed above the understanding of man; yet if miserable superstition still prevails in so many parts of the world, the blame must be attributed in no small measure to religious dissensions. For, as far as it is given to human reason to judge from the nature of events, this seems without doubt to be the mission assigned by God to Europe, to go on by degrees carrying Christian civilisation to every portion of the earth. The beginnings and first growth of this great work, which sprang from the labours of former centuries, were rapidly receiving large development, when all of a sudden the discord of the sixteenth century broke out. Christendom was torn with quarrels and dissensions, Europe exhausted with contests and wars, and the sacred missions felt the baneful influence of the times. While the causes of dissension still remain, what wonder is it that so large a portion of mankind is held enthralled with barbarous customs and insane rites?

All should labour for Unity. Let us one and all, then, for the sake of the common welfare, labour with equal assiduity to restore the ancient concord. In order to bring about this concord, and spread abroad the benefits of the Christian revelation, the present is the most seasonable time; for never before have the sentiments of human brotherhood penetrated so deeply into the souls of men, and never in any age has man been seen to seek out his fellow men more eagerly, in order to know them better and to help them. Immense tracts of land and sea are traversed with incredible rapidity, and thus extraordinary advantages are afforded, not only for commerce and scientific investigations, but also for the propagation of the word of God from the rising of the sun to the going down of the same.

We are well aware of the long labours involved in the restoration of that order of things which We desire; and it may be that there are those who consider that We are far too sanguine and look for things that are rather to be wished for than expected. But We unhesitatingly place all Our hope and confidence in the Saviour of mankind, Jesus Christ, well remembering what great things have been achieved in times past by the folly of the Cross and its preaching, to the astonishment and confusion of the *wisdom of the world.* We beg of princes and rulers of States, appealing to their statesmanship and earnest solicitude for the people, to weigh Our counsels in the balance of truth and second them with their authority and favour. If only a portion of the looked-for results should come about, it will cause no inconsiderable boon in the general decadence, when the intolerable evils of the present day bring with them the dread of further evils in days to come.

The last years of the past century left Europe worn out with disasters, and panic-stricken with the turmoils of revolution. And why should not our present century, which is now hastening to its close, by a reversion of circumstances bequeath to mankind the pledges of concord, with the prospects of the great benefits which are bound up in the unity of the Christian faith?

May God, Who *is rich in mercy, and in Whose power are the times and moments,* grant Our wishes and desires, and in His great goodness hasten the fulfilment of that divine promise of Jesus Christ: *There will be one Fold and one Shepherd.*

www.ingramcontent.com/pod-product-compliance
Lightning Source LLC
Chambersburg PA
CBHW031937230426
43672CB00010B/1950